*O*nce upon a time there was a kingdom without a king. This is how it came to be that a lively English princess and a distinguished Danish prince came to be crowned its king and queen, and how their son and his descendants came to be Norway's royal family . . . .

THE NORWEGIAN ROYAL FAMILY

B Y

Patricia C. Bjaaland

TANO

ISBN 82-518-2201-7
Engers Boktrykkeri A/S, Otta

Contents

THE PRINCESS

The English princess was little Princess Maud, the youngest of King Edward VII and Queen Alexandra's five children. As a young girl she was so shy that she was often teased. 'Her Royal Shyness,' however, was clearly no shrinking violet. She was one of the first members of the English aristocracy to take up the new sport of bicycling. When grandmother, the renowned Queen Victoria, protested on moral grounds, Maud is said to have responded, 'Grandmother, everyone knows I have legs!' The crisis was resolved by the use of bicycle clips.

Maud Charlotte Mary Victoria was born on November 26, 1869 and was christened on Christmas Eve of the same year at Marlborough House in London. Queen Victoria was present at the christening, wearing one of the black silk dresses she always wore after her beloved Albert's death.

Maud was born into no dull family. Her father's marriage to a Danish princess had been arranged after much deliberation, and although he was said to have a roving eye and gaming hand, the Prince and Princess of Wales had a happy and mutually satisfying marriage. Maud's mother was an extraordinary person with a strong natural presence and inner strength, and she regarded her husband's private pursuits as none of her business. While he tended to his affairs, she raised her five children. Then there was grandmother – Queen Victoria – an outspoken, if not meddlesome, and awesome woman. It's easy to understand how the youngest child of this colourful family might have seemed quiet in comparison. Time, however, brought Maud into her own.

Princess Maud and her two sisters, Louise and Victoria, were educated as befitted young princesses of Victorian England. The year after she was born, her family moved to Sandringham House in Norfolk, and it was there that she was raised. At the age of five, Maud began classes in 'Reception,' where she was taught social graces and how to meet strangers and put them at ease. She became an excellent horsewoman and rode daily whenever possible right up until her death. As an adolescent, she often visited friends incognito under the alias 'Miss Mills.' She loved both nature and animals and liked nothing more than a good frolic in the country with a faithful dog or two at her heels. She always enjoyed a good adventure – a trait she retained all her years. Her mother took to calling her by the pet name, 'Harry,' after a notorious friend of the family, Sir Henry (Harry) Keppel, who feared nothing. The name stuck for life.

Being a princess, however, wasn't always an enviable position. There was no question of attending regular schools, and there were few outings beyond the grounds of Sandringham in quiet West Norfolk. The Princess of Wales' annual holiday excursions, which often included the children, were thus welcomed diversions.

In 1893, Maud accompanied her mother and sister, Victoria, on a northern cruise. They visited the southern Norwegian coast on the royal yacht *Osborne* and even bought themselves Norwegian national dresses *(bunads)* from the Hardanger area as souvenirs. On August 31, Maud signed the guestbook at Oscarshall, a small neo–Gothic pleasure palace overlooking Oslo harbour, built in the time of King Oscar I (1799–1850). From Norway, the party continued on to Denmark for an annual family re-union at Maud's grandfather's, King Christian IX of Denmark.

As the years passed and Maud grew into an attractive young woman, the question of a suitable marriage arose. After her sister Louise's marriage, Maud's paternal aunt, mother of the German kaiser, wrote to Queen Victoria to recommend several German princes for her two marriageable nieces. Maud's Danish mother, however, had grown up under the shadow of German/Danish hostilities and was aghast at the proposal. No daughter of hers would marry a German! Other suitors were named, including an elderly English widower, but the Princess of Wales always found reasons for rejecting them. In the end, Maud's older sister Victoria ('Toria') never did marry, and to her mother's great joy, it was a Danish prince who won Maud's heart and hand.

THE SAILOR PRINCE

Prince Carl was born on Saturday afternoon, August 3, 1872. He was the third child born to the crown prince and princess of Denmark. His older brother, Christian, heir to the throne, had been born in 1870, and his sister, Louise, in 1871. A number of other siblings soon followed: Harald (b. 1876), Ingeborg (b. 1878), Thyra (b. 1880), Gustav (b. 1887), and finally Dagmar (b. 1890). Crown Prince Frederik (subsequently crowned as Frederik VIII) and Louise Josefina Eugenia were to have eight children in all.

Although baptized as Christian Frederik Carl Georg Valdemar Axel, at home he was known as Prince Carl. His father was the eldest of six children born to King Christian IX, a popular regent and respected figure of the times. His mother, the daughter of King Carl XV of Sweden and Norway, had married her husband when she was only seventeen, and was a good, and religious woman. During the winter his family lived at Amalienborg Palace in Copenhagen, and in the summer, they moved to Charlottenlund, north of the city, where Prince Carl was born. His first playmates were his older brother and sister.

The two elder sons were raised together and educated according to the norms of the time. Every morning they were awakened early to accompany their father on his 7 a.m. walk. After breakfast, their tutor arrived, and the day was filled with lessons and sports – Carl was said to be especially proficient at swimming and riding – and the cultivation of Christian virtues. Discipline was strict, but not overly so, and all the children were imbued with a strong sense of duty and responsibility. Bedtime was at 9 p.m. In 1887, when Christian was seventeen and Carl almost fifteen, they were confirmed.

The Danish prince destined to sit on Norway's throne, in 1885 at the age of 13. Although baptized as Christian Frederik Carl Georg Valdemar Axel, as a schoolboy he was known as Prince Carl at home (after his maternal grandfather) and as 'Charles' to his English relatives.

Throughout his childhood, Prince Carl had dreamed of going to sea and becoming a naval officer like his Uncle Waldemar. As a young boy, he had begged his mother to be allowed to have an anchor tatooed on his arm so ardently that she had eventually consented. Now, after his confirmation, he got his wish. He went to sea for nine months – as was the practice – to test his suitability. He passed, and within a year he was a cadet. Six years later, after a vigorous training program that included both theory and practice, he graduated with the rank of second lieutenant.

Prince Carl's decision to pursue a naval career was no surprise. A crown prince's destiny was certain; siblings had to find suitable careers. Most chose the military. Fortunately, the choice suited Prince Carl. Once, while in command of an elderly ship, a particularly demanding admiral was expected on an inspection tour. Prince Carl's second-in-command reported that all was in order. 'Have you polished the galley key?' he was asked. No, but it would be done immediately. The admiral arrived and poked and peeked while the crew, scrubbed and stiff, stood at attention. Eventually, the admiral approached the galley door, stretched out his arm, and removed the key from the keyhole. He had to nod his approval; he had met his match.

Prince Carl's years at sea took him to a number of ports ranging from the West Indies to St. Petersburg. Once, during a stop at Cadiz, Prince Carl and two fellow cadets decided to have their fortunes told. His friends went in first. When it was Carl's turn, the fortune teller examined his palm, hesitated, then predicted, 'You will be a king.' A sceptical Carl asked her to tell him about his past, but she refused, explaining that only the future could be told from a palm, not the past. Prince Carl had put in at Norway twice – both times at the port of Arendal on Norway's southern coast – but no fortune teller then had predicted he would one day return as the country's king.

When serving in the navy, Prince Carl refused to let his noble birth give him any advantage. He lived, ate, and worked as the other cadets did during his training years and worked his way up the hierarchy at his own pace. It took him three years to be promoted from the rank of second lieutenant to first lieutenant – and when asked why it had taken so long, joked that it was probably because he lacked the right connections. (In 1905, when he was being considered for Norway's empty throne, he was promoted to captain. He commented at the time that it was most likely because it hardly seemed fitting to ask a first lieutenant to be king!)

When not at sea, he lived at home with his parents at Amalienborg, where he had his own two-room bachelor suite. Whenever his schedule permitted, he attended dinner parties and reunions with the rest of the family at his grandfather's.

His famous grandfather, Christian IX of Denmark, was known as 'Europe's father-in-law,' and his summer house, Fredensborg, as 'Europe's parlour.' Through that parlour and on those lawns passed most of the crowned heads of Europe. Many were descended directly from him and his wife Louise (although she was far too retiring to ever be referred to as 'Europe's mother-in-law'). In addition to Carl's father (Fredrik VIII) and Maud's mother (Alexandra), they had a son (Wilhelm) who became King George of Greece, a daughter (Marie Dagmar) who became Czaress of Russia, another daughter (Thyra) who married the Duke of Cumberland, and a son (Waldemar) who married Princess Marie of Orleans and was offered the throne of Bulgaria (he did not accept). Family reunions at Fredensborg brought together most of his children, and in turn, their children.

The trim Princess Maud was well-known to her tall Danish cousin from family reunions at 'grandfather's.' It was reportedly at the family get-together in 1892 that the two young people formed their first attachment, which was rekindled at the following year's get-together after Maud's trip to Norway with her mother and sister. According to one of Prince Carl's commanding officers, the young cadet kept a photograph of his cousin hidden at the bottom of his drawer throughout his student years.

When 'Charles' (as his English relatives called him) proposed in 1895, Maud accepted at once. In January of 1896, she wrote in a letter, 'Charles really liked me 3 years but I never thought that it would last & that he would forget everything when he went to sea, but instead of that when he met me in the autumn again it became more so, & finally ended in this happy way!' Both her parents, the Prince and Princess of Wales, and her grandmother, Queen Victoria, approved. ('Hope shortly to make the acquaintance of my future grandson,' she telegraphed to Maud's parents when they sought her approval.) Popular opinion in England was more cautious. After all, England would be losing one of its favourite princesses, and the bridegroom seemed to have a limited future. Little was known about the prince, but the little that was, was positive, most acquiesced. And he was a naval officer – which was worth something.

Prince Carl married his beloved Maud on July 22, 1896 in the chapel of Buckingham Palace in London, under the approving eyes of Maud's grandmother, Queen Victoria, and both families. The bride wore her mother's veil. Once more it adorned a bride in an Anglo-Danish wedding: in 1863 it was the Danish Princess Alexandra who had married an English prince; now it was the English Princess Maud who was marrying a Danish prince. The wedding was the social event of the season.

Among Maud's wedding presents was her own residence on the grounds of Sandringham Castle in Norfolk. Appleton House was given to her by her father, the Prince of Wales, who had always had a special place in his heart for his youngest daughter, born nine months after his and Alexandra's fabled trip to the Near East (the trip of 'a thousand and one nights') in 1869.

Appleton House was to remain Maud's English home until she died, when it reverted to the English crown. Immediately after the London wedding ceremony and reception, Carl and Maud travelled by special train to Sandringham, where a dinner and ball for 1200 guests had been arranged. In distant Copenhagen, the streets were decorated with flags to celebrate the wedding of a Danish prince.

There was no honeymoon. The newlyweds chose, instead, to spend the first months of their marriage in Maud's beloved England. Denmark had to wait until Christmastime before the young couple moved into their new home in Copenhagen. They lived modestly on the first floor of a house on busy Bredgade owned by Prince Carl's uncle, the former Prince Wilhelm of Denmark, who now had little use for it as King George of Greece. Maud decorated the ten-room apartment in the style of the time, filling it with her collection of family photographs and the *objets d'art* that were so popular in Victorian England. The second floor was occupied by the Danish Supreme Court. On July 2, 1903, Maud gave birth to their one and only child, a son, at Appleton House in England. He was christened Alexander Edward Christian Frederik, in honour of his maternal grandmother, in the Sandringham chapel.

THE COUNTRY WITHOUT A KING OF ITS OWN

It is always difficult to pinpoint the exact historic moment where one can say, 'it all began.' This story is no exception. Norway was a patchwork of small Viking kingdoms until King Harald Hårfagre defeated the last major chieftains at the Battle of Hafrsfjord (approximately 900 A.D.) and unified the land. His heirs continued to strengthen and expand the kingdom, and Norway grew in both wealth and power. In 1349, however, disaster struck. The Black Death swept through Norway and left one-half to two-thirds of the population dead in its wake. Norway's economy, totally dependent upon the labour-heavy industries of fishing and farming, failed.

Meanwhile, intermarriage between the ruling families of Sweden, Norway, and Denmark eventually resulted in a united monarchy of the three countries. Sweden rebelled and managed to withdraw during the early 1400s, but Norway's weakened state left her unable to shake off Danish domination. From 1380 until 1814, Danish kings ruled over Norway, and Norway fell game to Danish and German exploitation.

In the early 1800s, Denmark allied itself with Napoleon and, in consequence, lost Norway. The Peace of Kiel in 1814 awarded Norway to Sweden as a trophy of war, but by then, Norway had ideas of its own. The rising cry of nationalism, stirred on by the ideas of the American and French revolutions, had given birth to a Norwegian movement for independence. A national assembly was called together at Eidsvoll, a manor in southern central Norway where the Norwegian Constitution was drafted. It was signed on May 17th, thereby establishing Norway's most beloved national holiday.

Among the demands of the Norwegian national assembly was that of an autonomous monarchy. The Danish Crown Prince Christian Frederik, one of the Norwegian independence movement's most eloquent spokesmen, was chosen by the assembly as Norway's new king, but Sweden responded to this burst of independence by invading Norway. Given the choice of war or union, Norway chose union with Sweden, and the elected regent was forced to withdraw. On November 4, 1814, the Norwegian parliament accepted Prince Christian Frederik's resignation and accepted union with Sweden under a new joint monarchy, this time under the rule of the 66-year-old King Karl XIII. (The deposed Christian Frederik went on to succeed his father as King of Denmark under the title King Christian VIII.)

Contention between Norway and Sweden over the Norwegian Constitution brewed throughout the union's ninety-one years of existence. Because the joint monarchy was the most obvious institution uniting the two countries, it became a focal point of the controversy. In 1893, a British journalist stationed in Berlin reported a plan calling for the dissolution of the Norwegian-Swedish union and the establishment of Prince Waldemar of Denmark as king of Norway. A flurry of letters, responses, speeches, proposals, and lists of possible regents followed: the issue of an independent Norway was out in the open, and one of the major questions was who would sit on the Norwegian throne.

At first, popular sentiment supported a member of the Swedish royal house, and one of the natural candidates was Prince Carl of Sweden (popularly known as the 'blue prince', married to Princess Ingeborg of Denmark). Although he was King Oscar II's son, he was not heir to the Norwegian-Swedish throne and was thus 'eligible.' The candidacy of a Swedish prince, however, did not close the issue, and other names began to be discussed in the cigar-

17

smoke-filled drawing rooms of Europe. A second Prince Carl, the second son of Denmark's crown prince, was among them.

By May 1905, it was clear that a break between Sweden and Norway was inevitable. On June 7, the formal message dissolving the union between the two countries was read aloud in the Norwegian parliament. There was no debate on the house floor. As the news raced throughout Norway, the union flag was lowered and the Norwegian flag raised in its place.

The aging King Oscar II was both shattered and furious at the news and vigorously protested the Norwegian decision. It was too late. Two weeks later, in a general plebiscite, Norway voted 368,208 votes in favour of dissolution, 184 against. Two months later, Oscar II relinquished the Norwegian crown.

Norway's throne now stood empty. It had not been filled by a Norwegian-born king for more than five centuries. The excitement that raced throughout the country can hardly be exaggerated. The search for a new king was on. Fredrik (Fritz) Wedel Jarlsberg, a Norwegian diplomat stationed in Madrid who circulated in Europe's inner circles, resigned his post and offered the fledgling nation his services.

Prince Carl of Denmark – King Haakon VII of Norway

NORWAY GAINS A KING AND QUEEN

While Europe waited to hear King Oscar II's pronouncement on the proposal that a Swedish prince assume the vacant Norwegian throne, Wedel Jarlsberg was hard at work. He had another ruling house in mind. What better candidate, he argued, than a Danish prince with ancestral ties to the Norwegian throne, who could already speak a Scandinavian language, who was united through an English wife to the English crown, and who had a young male heir to secure the line of succession? There could be no better candidate, argued Wedel Jarlsberg, than Prince Carl of Denmark.

Maud's father, Edward VII, was delighted with the idea when it was first whispered in his ear during that spring's Ascot Races, and he unofficially urged his son-in-law's case, confident that both the prince and his daughter would make regents that the Norwegian people would come to love and be proud of. At the same time, he sent a secret emissary to his daughter and son-in-law, who had just returned from an Aegean cruise with their young son, to urge them to accept the position if offered.

Prince Carl's first reaction was negative. His wife had never been happy in Denmark, but they had been discussing a move to England. Furthermore, he was content to be a naval officer – he had no personal ambition to become king of Norway. He was also concerned about his family's future lack of privacy. It took some time before the 32-year-old prince acquiesced.

A few weeks later, Prince Carl of Denmark was 'officially' summoned to a secret meeting with Norway's envoy, Wedel Jarlsberg. He waited until it was dark before slipping out of his Bredgade apartment and bicycling to the historic meeting. The date was Thursday, June 29th, 1905. Wedel Jarlsberg, prepared to argue with a reticent candidate, was overjoyed at the prince's willingness to accept. Before he had opened his mouth in greeting, Prince Carl openly and without false modesty, indicated his readiness to assume the Norwegian throne – on the understanding that he had not sought the position for himself, and the condition that, in his own words, 'You take me as I am.'

There was still the problem, however, of Sweden. There could be no question of a Danish prince accepting the post until it was quite clear that Sweden had relinquished all claims to it. The suspense seemed to go on forever until finally, on July 4, Prince Carl's father received a letter from Sweden's Oscar II: 'It would be difficult for me to allow any of my sons to accept the Norwegian crown.' Pressure was exerted on Prince Carl to travel to Norway immediately, but he refused, saying that he first had to receive his grandfather's blessing. A cautious Christian IX, however, felt compelled to wait for Oscar II's *official* declination. Despite further pressure from his father-in-law, Britain's King Edward VII, Prince Carl waited. He was promoted to captain in the Danish navy and carried on his sea duties as usual. Finally, on October 26, King Oscar II resignedly penned his name onto the statement that absolved him of the title King of Norway and Sweden.

Only one issue remained unresolved. In Norway, not everyone was convinced that Norway needed a king. In fact, the question of a republic for Norway was as old as the country's fight for independence, and the names of a number of prestigious Norwegians had been put forth as possible presidential candidates. The issue of a constitutional monarchy or a republic had to be put to rest.

On November 12 and 13, a plebiscite to settle the question was held in Norway at the express request of Prince Carl. The Danish prince had to ensure that he would be the people's choice, and not just one party's candidate: 'My task must above all be to unite, not to divide.' The final

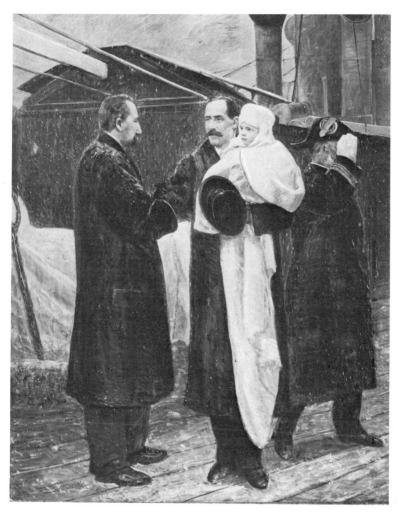

Halfdan Strøm's famous painting from 1930 depicting Norway's future King Haakon VII and Prime Minister Christian Michelsen on board the Heimdal *in Oslo fjord. Michelsen had waited on board the* Heimdal *to greet the royal party when they transferred over from the* Dannebrog *on the historic foggy morning of November 25, 1905. The picture was painted from a photograph and today hangs in the royal palace in Oslo.*

vote was 259,563 for a monarchy, 69,264 for a republic. The mandate of the people had been given.

On Saturday, November 18 the Norwegian parliament unanimously elected Prince Carl of Denmark King of Norway. He cabled back his immediate acceptance under the new name of Haakon VII, the name he had consented to accept months before. It had been proposed that his son, Alexander, be named Harald, but Princess Maud had objected. The new crown prince was to be known as Olav. Two days later, on November 20, Prince Carl and family stood before Denmark's king and received his blessing.

Within days, Norway's new sovereigns were on board the Danish ship *Dannebrog* headed for Norway – Maud wanted to celebrate her birthday in her new home. They were accompanied by Wedel Jarlsberg and his wife, the only Norwegians who accompanied the new royal family enroute to Norway. When they departed from Copenhagen on the morning of November 23, 1905, thousands of Danes stood on the shores to see them off. They were escorted part of the way by both German and British ships.

The sea was rough during the crossing, and Wedel Jarlsberg wrote in his diary that it was only he, the king, and captain and crew who were to be found above deck until the ship entered Oslo fjord.

The party of five transferred over to the Norwegian ship *Heimdal* outside of Drøbak on the morning of the 25th. It was very foggy, and vision was extremely limited. The flag that King Haakon had chosen as his banner, the Norwegian red standard with a gold lion, was raised. The Norwegian Prime Minister, Christian Michelsen, greeted the royal party: 'For nearly 600 years the Norwegian people have not had their own king. Today, that has changed. Today, Norway's young king has come to build his future home in Norway's capital.' The two men shook hands. Crooked in his father's left arm, sheltered from the lightly falling snow, wearing a polar bear hat and swathed in white, was the two-year-old crown prince.

At 12:30, the cannons of Akershus Castle boomed as the

'Behold, I am a queen!' the former English princess wrote home to England three weeks after her arrival in Norway. Although regal and poised in everything she did, her personality also allowed for a warm, natural spontaneity. She loved her hobbies of photography and gardening and was an active sportswoman long before sports for women were fashionable.

Heimdal slipped alongside the Kristiania (Oslo) quay. The day was cold and foggy, and a light veil of snow covered the city. Church bells rang as the handsome couple stepped onto Norwegian soil. As they were driven through the city, Edvard Grieg and Bjørnstjerne Bjørnson watched the procession.

Maud had gotten her wish. She spent her birthday, Sunday, the 26th of November, in her new home. Flags waved throughout the city in her honour. That evening, they attended a dinner hosted by Prime Minister Michelsen. The next day, Haakon swore his oath of allegiance to the Norwegian constitution before the Norwegian parliament, and three weeks later Maud wrote home, 'Behold! I am a Queen!!'

One month after their first 17th of May celebration—when the little crown prince stole the populace's hearts by waving a Norwegian flag from his stroller—the royal family embarked on their coronation tour of Norway enroute to the cathedral city of Trondheim.

They departed on June 13, 1906 and travelled through Gudbrandsdalen and Romsdalen to Åndalsnes. From Åndalsnes they continued by boat to Trondheim via Molde and Kristiansund. There are still Norwegians who remember the coronation trip, including one woman who was then only a few years older than the crown prince. She had been chosen to present him with a bouquet of flowers. 'But I couldn't, his father was holding him, and he was too high up. At last, the king saw me reaching up with my flowers, but instead of lowering the prince, he reached down and took the bouquet himself. That was too much to bear. "It's not for you, it's for him!" I cried out!'

During his first months in Norway, the new king enjoyed walking about the streets undetected. One beautiful summer evening just before the coronation, Haakon slipped past the curious crowd that was constantly gathered outside his Trondheim residence. The entire city seemed to be out that evening, and after a while, he entered into casual conversation with another stroller. They had exchanged a few

24

'It all haunts me like a nightmare this Coronation & that it is to be ours of all people. Think of me alone on my throne having a crown . . . before the whole crowd. Gracious, it will be awful!' Maud wrote home to her brother before being crowned Queen of Norway on Friday, June 22, 1906 in the Nidaros Cathedral in Trondheim.

comments when the elderly man became curious. 'You sound Danish. Are you here for the coronation?' 'Yes,' was the modest response of Norway's new king.

On June 22, 1906 King Haakon VII and Queen Maud were crowned king and queen of Norway in Trondheim's Nidaros Cathedral. Norway once more had its own royal family.

It is said that God gives and God takes away. While gaining a king and queen, Norway lost one of its greatest sons. Almost exactly one month prior to the coronation, on May 23, Norway's most famous playwright, Henrik Ibsen, passed away.

THE LITTLE PRINCE

His parents may have been the star attraction on Kristiania's snowy quay when the *Heimdal* disembarked its famous passengers, but it wasn't long before the new crown prince had his share of attention, too. No one noticed the little two-year-old at first. There were many dignitaries; welcome speeches were being read; and the foul weather diverted one's attention. When Queen Maud noticed that her son was getting restless, she signalled to his nurse that he be put down. The young child stood still for a while, then toddled closer to the members of the welcoming committee. As the formal ceremony continued, the little prince smiled, caught a dignitary's eye, and waved. From then on, Norway's new crown prince took the city by storm.

The original plan for the family's procession into the capital city called for the little prince to ride in a closed car behind his parents' open carriage, but King Haakon quickly realized the folly of that decision. His son was an important symbol to the Norwegian people and belonged with his parents. Crown Prince Olav sat between them during the triumphal drive. The 25,000 bundled-up school children, who had stood shivering in the mist and fog to catch a glimpse of the youngest member of the new royal family, were not disappointed.

The symbolic strength of the crown prince was not to be underestimated. One of the newspaper accounts of the day reported that as the new king held his son in his arms on the balcony of the royal palace before the assembled crowd, the little prince had waved, and the sun had broken through the enveloping fog.

Crown Prince Olav, not yet three years old, photographed in Oslo's royal palace in 1906. He was so adored by the public that as a young child he had to be protected from the many well-wishers wanting either a hug or a handshake. Now well into his 80s, our 'People's King' is as popular as ever.

As a toddler, his daily walks had to be limited to the fenced-in 'Queen's Park' behind the palace due to all the admiring ladies wanting kisses. He was Norway's adored 'little prince,' and his picture hung on many a wallpapered, lace-curtained Norwegian drawing-room and schoolroom wall. Songs and poems in his honour flourished, and every magazine was adulatory in its language when it concerned the youngest member of the royal family. His parents may have been the king and queen, but all of Norway considered him theirs.

A family ski tour with friends. Crown Prince Olav, who received his first pair of skis at the age of three-and-a-half leads, followed by the family dog 'Ponto'. Mother and father, who had none other than the famous Fridtjof Nansen as ski instructor, and friends follow.

He was an appealing and active youngster, eager to try everything. It is no surprise that his earliest memory is of a piece of sports equipment – a sled he received for his third birthday, celebrated in Trondheim a week after his parents' coronation. The sled was a gift from the children of the city, and the lack of snow mid-summer didn't stop Norway's new crown prince from putting it into use at once – albeit in his nursery.

He was three-and-a-half-years old when he tried out his first pair of skis on the snow-covered lawn of the palace, and was such an eager pupil that there was many a day when it was hard getting them off him again! More than once, his ski instructor related, the little crown prince stomped back into the palace and down its long corridors with his skis still strapped to his feet. It wasn't long before he was able to join his parents on the slopes.

Life was full. If father was too busy to play, mother was usually available, or one of the many dogs always about. There was skiing, cricket, riding, lawn tennis, rowing, and sailing. Even the palace staff was called into duty. One day, Queen Maud snapped a photo of her son skipping rope with two palace guards.

Politicians, explorers, and adventurers were part of the crown prince's daily world. There were many visits from relatives and friends from abroad, as well as return visits. Queen Maud's mother and sister, Queen Alexandra and Princess Victoria, visited them during their first Norwegian summer, and later that autumn they visited King Haakon's family in Denmark. In 1908, just before his 5th birthday, both of Olav's maternal grandparents, King Edward VII and Queen Alexandra, visited Norway, accompanied by English cruisers. Two years later, in 1910, Teddy Roosevelt arrived to give his acceptance speech for the Nobel Peace Prize he had won in 1906. Famous and important guests were always coming and going, but the royal family was always to say that because there was just the three of them, they were an unusually close family.

One of the royal family's first visitors was the German kaiser, who had announced his intention to visit immediately following the coronation in Trondheim. He was very fond of the Norwegian coastline and spent several holidays cruising in the area. Although both he and Queen Maud were grandchildren of Queen Victoria and had always used English during family get-togethers, he demanded that German be spoken during his visit. Queen Maud was furious. It was King Haakon who saved the day. As the two monarchs sat side-by-side in King Haakon's carriage, King Haakon brought up the subject. 'Wilhelm, you know that letter you wrote saying that we should use German during your visit. . . .' 'Yes?' 'Well, my officers and Cabinet have been practising so hard that they've worn out all the German helping verbs. You know how hard it is finding new ones in such a small town as Trondheim. How about it. . .?' The kaiser laughed and relented. The visit was conducted in English.

Today, some of H.M. King Olav's fondest memories are those from his childhood years spent with his parents on the royal farm at Bygdøy. The property used to belong to a monastery in the 12th century, but it was situated so ideally on Bygdøy peninsula in Oslo harbour, that it was soon noticed by the king. It was eventually presented to Queen Eufemia by her husband, King Haakon V. Magnusson, in 1305. During the Middle Ages, it was used as a royal hunting lodge.

The farm was no elegant princely residence when it was first presented to Haakon and Maud in 1905, but that only seemed to make it dearer to them. Here was an idyllic summer residence where Olav could keep rabbits and pigeons, Maud her horses and dogs, and Haakon escape the demands of his office. Olav learned how to ride and row in the little pond while his mother rode or puttered in her beloved garden, often busily choosing plants to be transplanted to the grounds of Balmoral Castle in Scotland. In many ways, Bygdøy reminded Maud of her family home, Sandringham.

Thanks to Queen Maud's interest in amateur photography, there are many charming photographs of the family during their summers at Bygdøy Kongsgård. In addition to gardening and photography, the queen loved to read and keep scrapbooks, and it was rumoured that she played whist as skilfully as her fun-loving father, Edward VII. She was a lively and active woman, firm in her beliefs, who vigourously attacked anything she set out to do – whether it be redecorating the palace (she abhorred the plush furniture she found there and soon had it recovered) or establishing a fund to help the needy (Queen Maud's famous *Hjelpefond*)—and did it all with elegance and flair.

One of King Haakon's and Queen Maud's first activities in Norway the winter of 1905-1906 was to attend the famous Holmenkollen Ski Competition. Holmenkollbakken had been used for the first time just fifteen years earlier (January 31, 1892) when other sites had proven too limited for daredevil Norwegian jumpers. Unfortunately, it was a treacherous stormy day and as they bent their chins into their turned-up collars in the howling wind, they may have had second thoughts about the previous June's decision!

Crown Prince Olav was seven-years old when he attended the Holmenkollen ski-jumping competition for the first time in 1911. By then, Queen Maud must have decided that if you can't fight them, join them. As the family watched the jumpers, Queen Maud is said to have whispered to her son, 'One day you'll jump here, too.'

Crown Prince Olav's youth was spent under the shadow of World War I. The years were anxious ones, for the family feared not only for the fate of Norway, but also for family members spread over the face of Europe. Although neutral during the war, Norway's merchant marine was harassed by German submarines and over 2,000 of its sailors were lost. At home, its citizens experienced serious shortages of food and raw materials. In December 1914, King Haakon VII met with his brother, King Christian X of Denmark, and King Gustav V of Sweden in Malmø, Sweden to confirm the need for unity in this time of crisis. A similar meeting was held in Oslo (then still called Kristiania) three years later.

The crown prince was 15-years old when the war ended. In 1918, the same year he finished his primary school education and was confirmed, he won two third prizes in local ski-jumping competitions. This was to be his debut in the world of competitive skiing that peaked when he competed in the 1922 and 1923 Holmenkollen ski-jumping competitions, just as his mother had once predicted.

Queen Maud celebrated her 50th birthday in 1919. There were formal receptions and speeches, but her best present came four months before her November 26 birthday when a long-held wish was fulfilled: a ride in an airplane. The king was not amused. In another three years, when he celebrated his own 50th birthday, it was without such bravado. He never did go up in an airplane.

Skiing was a favorite pastime for the Norwegian royal family. The king had been introduced to the sport by none other than Fridtjof Nansen, one of Norway's most famous adventurers, renowned for crossing Greenland on skis. An American newspaper once carried a laudatory story on the skiing skills of the king and crown prince and came to the conclusion that they were an excellent illustration of the famous truism, 'Norwegians are born with skis on their feet.' Norwegians loved the story, knowing full well that their beloved king and crown prince had been born, respectively, in Denmark and England!

Queen Maud had never skied before she moved to Norway, but quickly made up for it. It became the family's practice to move up to 'The King's Chalet,' *Kongsseteren*, several weeks between Christmas and Easter. *Kongsseteren* had been presented to King Haakon and Queen Maud as a coronation present in 1906, and they came to love their Voksenåsen skiing and sledding retreat dearly. One day, when the king and queen were out skiing, they came to the top of a steep slope. A Swedish couple stood there, admiring the view. The king hesitated at the summit before pushing off, but Maud hurled down the hill. 'Look at that girl,' called out one of the tourists. 'Yes,' answered King Haakon, 'not bad considering she's sixty.'

In 1923, Crown Prince Olav was scheduled to participate in the Norwegian Championship at Songebakken outside Tvedestrand, but icy conditions had posed the question of the safety of the jump. 'If other Norwegian boys are going to jump, then the Crown Prince will, too,' announced Queen Maud. He did, and placed fourth in his class.

Schoolwork may have seemed tedious to the athletic youth, but he did well in his studies. He was tutored privately at home until he was old enough to enter secondary school. He did well at Hallings School, in Oslo, and was even elected editor of a student newspaper for a short

*The royal family at Bygdøy Kongsgård summer 1924, the summer
Crown Prince Olav celebrated his 21st birthday.*

while – until replaced as head of the organization by a student coup! He graduated in 1921, the same year his parents celebrated their silver wedding anniversary, and then went on to enter the Norwegian Military Academy.

Originally, Crown Prince Olav was to have attended the Military Academy for only one year, but he soon asked for permission to follow the three-year program to completion. His father consented.

Crown Prince Olav was still a cadet at the Military Academy on his 21st birthday, July 2, 1924, but he was granted leave that day and driven into Oslo. He attended his first cabinet meeting with his father and gave his oath of allegiance to the Norwegian constitution. The day was filled with formal calls and the presentation of birthday gifts and honours. One surprise gift that pleased him immensely was a gray Fiat Model 501, presented by the Royal Norwegian Automobile Club. (His father had learned to drive in 1913 and had been a confirmed driver ever since.)

A banquet that evening concluded the crown prince's birthday celebrations. There, a proud father thanked his son for a childhood that has 'never brought us a day's sorrow or worry' and referred to his son's decision to complete the full course of training at the Military Academy as evidence of Olav's understanding that 'doing things halfway in life isn't good enough.'

Among all the gifts the crown prince received on his 21st birthday, there was one that would be enjoyed by him and his family countless times throughout the years. 'The Prince's Chalet' *(Prinsehytta)* in Sikkilsdalen was presented to Crown Prince Olav by the two Swedish princes, Crown Prince Gustaf Adolf and Prince Wilhelm. It had belonged to all three of the Swedish princes (the youngest, Prince Erik, died at the end of the first World War) since the turn of the century, but had last been used in 1905, the year the union between Norway and Sweden had been dissolved. The chalet had been bought for the Swedish princes with money raised by the people of Norway when the King of Norway and Sweden, Oscar II, had sat on the throne. Crown Prince Olav was deeply moved by the present.

When he graduated from the Military Academy that autumn (fourth in his class), he immediately spent a few days at the new cabin in Gudbrandsdalen. The crown prince was able to use it only sporadically in the early years, but later, he and his family vacationed there whenever possible. It has been a favourite autumn hunting lodge and winter ski chalet of the Norwegian royal family ever since.

Later that autumn, on a rainy Saturday in October, 1924, Crown Prince Olav, accompanied by his mother, was enrolled at Balliol, Oxford's second oldest college, and one favoured by many a diplomat and scholar. His parents had requested that there be as little special attention paid to their son as possible, so the new student was able to settle in without too much ado. Queen Maud returned to Appleton House to visit with her mother, who would soon be celebrating her 80th birthday.

One afternoon towards the end of the crown prince's second autumn term, on November 20, 1925, the phone rang. It was Queen Maud, calling from Sandringham. His grandmother, Queen Alexandra, was dead. He left school the same evening and was by his mother's side at Sandringham the next day. A small memorial service for the family and close friends was held in the chapel in Sandringham, the same chapel that Crown Prince Olav had been baptized in 22 years before. The day Queen Alexandra was laid to rest, a light cover of new snow fell over London. The press found it symbolic that it had also snowed on the day Alexandra had arrived in London from Denmark as the Prince of Wales' bride in 1863.

Among the guests attending Queen Alexandra's funeral were representatives from most of Europe's ruling families. Two Swedish princesses, Märtha and Astrid, cousins of Crown Prince Olav, were also present. After the funeral, the crown prince returned to Oxford.

Days were filled with political science and economics, an occasional free hour spent over the newspapers or chatting in 'The Oxford Union,' and training at general athletics. Later he was to comment that the two winters he spent in England made it impossible for him to keep up his competitive skiing, but Crown Prince Olav filled part of the void with the traditional English sport of rowing.

Although an all-round sportsman, skiing held a special place in the heart of the crown prince. He had, after all, skied from the age of three. Rowing may have been demanding and interesting, and the meets certainly colourful and traditional, but it didn't hold up to his other love, either – sailing.

His first sailboat had a 22-square-meter sail and was called *Teddy*. It was a present from his parents on his 15th birthday, together with membership in the junior division of the Royal Norwegian Yacht Club. In time, the original

Teddy was replaced by another *Teddy,* and the crown prince had begun to prove himself as much born to the wind as to the slopes. When he acquired the 6-meter *Oslo* in 1925, a way of life had not only been born, but also baptized and confirmed.

Skiing and sailing have been the seasonal variants ever since. For years, the crown prince flew the Norwegian colours around the world in competitive events. One year after he became a qualified ski-jump judge, an ability which unfortunately has never been tested in an international meet, the Norwegian Olympic Committee entered his 6-meter boat, *Norna,* in the 1928 Olympics. Crown Prince Olav sailed in the crew and helped win Norway a gold medal. He won another prize for Norway during the 1928 Olympics – his future bride.

A NEW BRIDE FOR NORWAY'S ROYAL HOUSE

Crown Prince Olav had known his Swedish cousin since childhood. She had been born on March 28, 1901, the middle of three Swedish princesses. Her father was Prince Carl, the 'blue prince' who had been one of the most popular candidates for the Norwegian throne in 1905. When she was born, twenty-one shots had been fired in Norway marking the birth of the granddaughter of Oscar II, King of Norway and Sweden. Her mother was Princess Ingeborg, a Danish princess, and one of King Haakon VII's younger sisters.

Märtha Sofia Lovisa Dagmar Thyra grew up in Stockholm and spent her summers at the family's summer residence, Fridhem, together with her sisters, Margaretha and Astrid, and a younger brother, Carl. When she was two years old in 1903, she and her family visited Norway. The political break between Norway and Sweden in 1905, however, put a stop to any subsequent visits.

Her father was not destined for any throne, so her childhood was, in many ways, far freer than might have been. After a normal childhood education, the soft-eyed princess studied pediatric nursing, cooking and sewing. She was said to excel at all three: she had a natural ease with children, was a whiz with sauces, and more than one magazine of the time featured a picture of her in 'a fashionable self-sewn dress.'

The adjectives used to describe her always include such words as 'practical,' 'energetic,' 'kind,' 'altruistic,' and 'patient.' She was, in every respect, a lovely person. She was the type, it was once written, that looked people

Crown Prince Olav's future bride (Princess Märtha of Sweden, far right), at the age of nine, together with her mother (King Haakon VII's younger sister) and two sisters, in 1910. From left to right: Princess Margaretha, Princess Ingeborg, Princess Astrid, and Princess Märtha. Princess Märtha was christened Märtha Sophie Louise Dagmar Thyra. The latter four names were old family names, but the name she was to be known by, Märtha, was chosen by her father simply because he liked it.

directly in the eyes and really listened, and was 'not given to saying clever things that ended up in American newspaper headlines.'

Olav first really noticed his Swedish cousin's charming ways at his paternal grandmother's 70th-birthday party in Charlottenlund, Denmark, autumn 1921. He had just turned eighteen; his cousin Märtha was twenty. She and her sister and mother later visited his family at Bygdøy Kongsgård. These visits sparked rumours about a possible new Norwegian-Swedish alliance of a more private nature than that from 1814 to 1905, but nobody could guess which of the two Swedish princesses it might be. When Astrid's engagement to Belgium's Crown Prince Leopold was announced in 1926, more than a few speculators were surprised.

During the 1928 Summer Olympics in Amsterdam, the two cousins met again. Princess Märtha was visiting her sister, Astrid, in Brussels, as she often did. Crown Prince Olav was a member of the Norwegian Olympic team, representing Norway with his boat, the *Norna*. He had informed his parents of his intention before he had left home. When Märtha accepted, he cabled home, 'All in order.' He was twenty-five, she twenty-seven. They managed to keep their engagement a secret until its formal announcement on January 14, 1929. The crown prince travelled by train to Stockholm under the name Olav Håkonsson, undetected by those too slow-witted to unravel the name's true meaning – Olav, son of Haakon! The engagement was announced during his three-week visit.

Then came the second surprise. It was announced that the marriage of the Swedish princess to the Norwegian prince would *not* take place in Stockholm, as might be expected, but in Oslo. That was Queen Maud's idea, fully supported by her husband. For precedent, she cited the marriage of her own mother, who had travelled to London in 1863 to become the bride of the Prince of Wales. She knew what the first royal marriage in Norway in 340 years would mean to the populace. Sweden had had a monopoly over royal weddings in the past; now it was Norway's turn.

Crown Prince Olav's marriage to Princess Märtha was not only the first royal wedding to be held in Norway in 340 years, but also the first wedding of a Norwegian prince to be held in Norway in more than 600 years. Norway went wild.

They were to be married on March 21 in Vår Frelsers Church. King Haakon VII had regularly attended services there since his arrival in Norway. Queen Maud, on the other hand, attended services at the English Church. She disliked having to part ways with her husband Sunday

One of the many pictures taken of Crown Prince Olav and Princess Märtha after their engagement was announced, January 1929. Any doubts they may have harboured as to the popularity of a new Swedish-Norwegian alliance were quickly dispelled by the jubilant reception their betrothal received in both countries.

mornings, but she never felt at ease in Norwegian services, in part because her command of Norwegian was never that good.

Princess Märtha arrived in Oslo with her parents on

Tuesday, March 19. Crown Prince Olav and his father, in full dress, were awaiting their train when it arrived at 11:20 that morning. The first to emerge were the bride's parents – Prince Carl and Princess Ingeborg – and then the bride herself. She was wearing a seagreen coat with large white fur collar and matching seagreen cloche. Crown Prince Olav took her hand and the young couple walked hand-in-hand from the station to a waiting open carriage.

It was a perfect day – cool in the shade, but spring warm in the sun. As the betrothed couple rode through the streets of Oslo to the royal palace they were cheered by thousands of well-wishers in the tightly packed streets.

The city was totally festooned with flags, garlands, and the initials M and O entwined in red and gold. Thirty-six huge obelisks made of ice blocks lined the main street (Karl Johans Gate) leading up to the royal palace. Only the palace itself stood undecorated in the frenzy of wedding decorations.

They were married on Thursday, March 21, on a cold, foggy day that only got worse as the day progressed. Hardly a soul in Oslo noticed. The first spectators were on the streets the night before, and the sidewalks were packed by 8 a.m. Peddlars hawked wooden cases to stand on. The first wedding guests began to arrive at Vår Frelsers Church at 10:00. At 11:50 Crown Prince Olav and his best man, the Duke of York, arrived. At 12:02 the bride and her father arrived.

The newlyweds emerged a little before 1:00. Forty-two rounds (a 'double' royal salute) were sounded from Akershus Castle, and the crowd exploded in excitement. Hats and handkerchiefs were waved, handfuls of rice thrown into the air, and a continual thunder of hurrahs released from the jubilant onlookers.

After the wedding luncheon, the couple rode through the city for three hours in a four-hourse state carriage. There was no limit to the joy they created wherever they were driven. Children had dressed themselves in the red, white, and blue of the Norwegian flag and yellow and blue of the

Swedish flag with the letters M and O on their chests. At Schous Brewery, two older employees who had been elected to present bouquets to the newlyweds waited by the brewery's gates. As the carriage rolled by, they were too overcome to move. Other bouquets reached the newlyweds, however, and when the carriage returned to the palace, it was overflowing with flowers.

As evening approached, the street lights on Oslo's main street were turned off, and the gas lights on the ice obelisks lit. There was a beautiful romantic glow to the sky, enhanced by a dramatic unplanned fire that swept Oslo's largest department store and destroyed all five stories. As the couple sped away by train to Cannes and the Riviera for the first part of their honeymoon, the palace musicians tuned their instruments. The strains of ball music lasted far into the fairy-tale night.

THE NEW FAMILY

When Crown Prince Olav announced his engagement to his Swedish cousin, Princess Märtha, all of Norway assumed that the couple would reside at Oscarshall, the small, if slightly run-down, 'pleasure palace' overlooking Oslo harbour that had been built at the initiative of King Oscar I (1799-1850). Plans for remodelling it had been in the air for years. Prior to the crown prince's engagement, King Haakon VII had opened the grounds to the public on the condition that Oscarshall revert to the crown whenever so needed.

It was not to be, however. One month after Crown Prince Olav and Princess Märtha announced their engagement, the Swedish newspaper *Svenska Dagbladet* reported the crown prince as saying that if he and his bride were expected to reside in either the royal palace or Oscarshall, he preferred a 3-room apartment in Oslo instead. When the royal couple departed on their honeymoon, the problem of a permanent residence still hadn't been solved.

Fortunately, the choice never had to be made, for among their belated wedding presents was the perfect residence – Skaugum.

Skaugum was a magnificent estate, located only 20 kilometers outside of Oslo, which belonged to Wedel Jarlsberg, now an old friend of the royal family. He had known Crown Prince Olav since he was a young child, and the crown prince and his new bride had stopped in to visit him in Paris during their honeymoon. When he heard that a suitable residence still hadn't been found, he wrote H.M. King Haakon VII and offered Skaugum.

Skaugum was a historic old farm dating back to the 14th century. It had originally belonged to the Church of Mary in Oslo, but had changed ownership several times before it was bought by Wedel Jarlsberg in 1909. The house was well-known. Crown Princess Märtha's father had even been a houseguest there in 1890. Wedel Jarlsberg presented the estate with all its possessions intact – the only items removed were a few personal paintings, photographs and memorabilia.

The newlyweds moved in on October 12, 1929 and began to decorate the house to their own tastes. Crown Princess Märtha's uncle even visited them to offer his advice. Within eight months, however, on May 21, 1930, a tragedy occured that forced them out of their beautiful new home.

The royal couple had been working long hours readying the house for the birth of their first child, due in a few weeks. One evening, as the crown prince was hanging a picture, he noticed smoke. He went outside to look for its source and discovered the entire attic in flames. Luckily, the fire was discovered early enough so that most of the house's possessions were saved although the house itself was gutted. That evening, when the crown princess drove into town for the night, her new pink baby bassinet was with her in the car.

The day after Skaugum burned down, an architect was consulted, and plans for the rebuilding and remodelling of the house were set into motion. Shortly after, however, the nation's attention was diverted by the birth of the first royal child in Norway since the Middle Ages.

Princess Ragnhild Alexandra was born at 3:10 p.m. on June 9, 1930 in the royal palace, where her parents had been living since the fire at Skaugum. Queen Maud was redecorating Appleton House at the time and was so pleased that she immediately included plans for a new nursery for her granddaughter.

There were many Ragnhilds in Norwegian history, but the most famous was Queen Ragnhild, the daughter of a local king from Ringerike who, according to Snorre's *Sagas*, was rescued from an abductor by Halvdan Svarte. She later married him and one night dreamed that the tree she lay under grew and blossomed until it covered all of Norway. Her son, Harald Hårfagre, was the king who united Norway, and his progeny did come to rule the country. When he, in turn, married for the third time, he chose another Ragnhild. She was a Danish princess and the first foreign bride to marry into the Norwegian royal family.

Princess Ragnhild was baptized two weeks later in the palace chapel, the first time a Norwegian princess had ever been baptized there. Her grandmother, Queen Maud, carried her to the baptismal font. Twenty months later, a second daughter was born to the crown prince and princess.

Princess Astrid Maud Ingeborg was born on February 12, 1932 at Solbakken, a temporary residence the crown prince and his family lived in while awaiting the completion of Skaugum. She was named in honour of Princess Märtha's sister, Princess Astrid of Sweden, married to the Belgian crown prince and Belgium's future queen. Maud and Ingeborg were the little princess' paternal and maternal grandmothers' names.

The completion of Skaugum took much longer than originally estimated, and when the crown prince and princess were able to move back in, they were a family of four with a two-year-old and a six-month-old baby. The date was August 2, 1932, the day before King Haakon's 60th birthday. Just a week before it hadn't seemed possible that the house could be readied in time. None of the furniture had even been moved in. But everyone knew how much the crown prince and his family wanted to celebrate the king's birthday at Skaugum, so volunteer crews had worked round-the-clock to make it possible.

Five years later, on a cold, February day, their third child, a boy, was born. Since 1260 A.D. Norway has recognized the eldest legitimate son of a king as the rightful successor to the throne. The little prince, the only royal child to be born at Skaugum, thus became Norway's newest royal heir, destined one day to follow his father to the throne. His sisters, Astrid and Ragnhild, were sent outside to play while awaiting the birth of their new sibling. Five-

Crown Princess Märtha with her Swedish family at their Stockholm home, summer 1935. From left to right: Princess Margaretha (married to the Danish Prince Axel), Prince Carl (junior), Crown Princess Märtha of Norway and her father Prince Carl, Queen Astrid (married to king Leopold of Belgium), and Princess Ingeborg.

year-old Astrid's response, when told about her new brother, was recorded throughout the land: 'Can he come out and play with us in the snow, too?'

Astrid and Ragnhild's baby brother was born midday on Sunday, February 21, 1937. Newspapers are forbidden on Sundays in Norway (a law meant to protect workers), but an exception was made on that Sunday. Excited historians had worked out that it had been 567 years since the previous birth of a Norwegian prince in Norway. (The Norwegian prince born 567 years before had been named Olav, and was the son of Queen Margrete and King Haakon

Their royal highnesses King Haakon VII, Crown Prince Olav, Queen Maud, and Crown Princess Märtha attending a function at the Royal Norwegian Yacht Club in 1935. To the delight of this maritime nation, members of the Norwegian royal family have always been keen sailors. H.M. King Haakon VII was a captain in the Danish navy, and both his son and grandson inherited his love of the sea—albeit on more recreational grounds. Both H.M. King Olav V and Crown Prince Harald and Crown Princess Sonja have won numerous competitive sailing events.

VI.) Genealogists quickly traced the little heir's lineage back 32 generations to Norway's first king, Harald Hårfagre.

The newest addition to the crown prince's family was named Harald, the very name proposed for Olav 32 years before when he was still little Prince Alexander of Denmark. When Harald assumes the throne, he will be the fifth Harald to reign in Norway, following Harald Hårfagre

Crown Prince Olav and his family, 1937. The crown prince had grown up in Norway as an only child, but with his marriage, Norway's citizens were treated to the joy of a trio of royal children to dote over. Princess Ragnhild was born in 1930, Princess Astrid in 1932, and Prince Harald in 1937. Although Harald was the last of the three to be born, he was next in line of succession after his father inasmuch as Norway only recognizes the agnatisk (or male line) of succession.

(Norway's unifier), Harald Gråfell (son of Eirik Blodøks), Harald Hardråde (the founder of Oslo), and Harald Gille (who was born in Ireland as a Gilchrist).

All three of Olav and Märtha's children were baptized in a gown handmade in 1899 by Queen Ingeborg of Denmark, Haakon VII's sister and Crown Princess Märtha's mother, which has been used for baptisms in the Norwegian royal family ever since. Queen Maud carried her youngest grandchild to the baptismal font in the palace's chapel, but she died before his second birthday.

THE LOSS OF A QUEEN

Each autumn as the first signs of winter fell over Norway, Queen Maud would return home to England. She had always done so, even when she was a young bride living in Denmark. When King Haakon VII was first approached as a royal candidate in Copenhagen in 1905, he had voiced his fear that his wife's frequent trips to England might be misunderstood. In time, Norwegians came to understand that Queen Maud's trips home were not from a lack of love for Norway, but from another, equally deep love for her own homeland.

Queen Maud (centre) was, in every respect, a very sporty lady.

The crown prince's residence, Skaugum, located in Asker, outside of Oslo, was—and still is—a perfect place for children to grow up. Its lush grounds offer a healthy, natural environment that has now served two generations of royal children. Today, Princess Märtha Louise and Prince Haakon Magnus play on the same grounds where their father and his two sisters played fifty years ago.

When Queen Maud was in England, she called on old friends, visited with her family, shopped for English gifts to bring back to Norway, presented English friends with Norwegian gifts, and did all the little errands she had saved up since the last visit. When not in London, she resided at Appleton House. Crown Prince Olav and Märtha's honeymoon had included a stay at Appleton House, 'Olav & Märtha are with me now, having arrived yesterday by car, looking very well and radiantly happy,' she wrote to Queen Mary at the time. They returned home to Norway with Queen Maud just in time for Crown Princess Märtha's first Norwegian 17th of May.

Queen Maud's trip home in the fall of 1938 began no differently than any other trip. The first warning given the

50

public was a small notice that appeared in the Norwegian newspaper *Aftenposten* on Monday, November 14. The article was short and to the point: 'Queen Maud Ill. King travels this evening to London.' Six days later she died quietly in her sleep, following an operation. She was taken to the chapel at Marlborough House, then, accompanied by husband and son, to Victoria Station in London where a special train bore her coffin to Portsmouth. The English ship *Royal Oak* brought her home to Norway. Her funeral service was held in the same church she watched her only child married in a decade before. Today, her casket lies in the royal crypt under Akershus Chapel. She was such an active and lively person that few Norwegians even today realize that she was only one year short of turning seventy when she died.

THE MONARCHY

In his youth, Crown Prince Olav occasionally accompanied his father to the opening of a new railroad line or the christening of a ship, but the crown prince was allowed to live as private a life as possible during his early years. As a student at Balliol, he had laid the foundation stone for the Norwegian Seamen's Church in London, but this was the exception that proved the rule. As he reached adulthood, he began to assume those responsibilities required of him, but an effort was made to ensure that he and his family had a private life of their own, too. Although both the crown prince and princess were busy representing Norway on many an official occasion, private photographs of the royal family reflect a radiant couple surrounded by their three active and healthy children.

One of the most important trips the crown prince and princess embarked on was their famous America tour in the spring of 1939. Crown Prince Olav and Crown Princess Märtha's tour of Norwegian America not only strengthened the official bonds between the two countries, but also gave hundreds of thousands of Norwegian-Americans the opportunity to greet 'their' prince and princess.

On April 19, 1939 Ragnhild, Astrid, and Harald were left under the watchful eye of their grandfather while the crown prince and princess departed for America on board the *Oslofjord*. From the day they arrived in New York harbour, April 27, until they returned home to Norway on the *Stavangerfjord* July 17, the royal couple was overwhelmed by American hospitality and enthusiasm. They were the personal guests of the Roosevelts. They were made honorary members of Indian tribes. They were

Crown Prince Olav and Crown Princess Märtha's America Tour in 1939 not only cemented an offical friendship between the two nations, but also a personal friendship between the American president and Norway's ruling house. During their visit to the 'Summer White House,' (Hyde Park, New York), the crown prince and princess were fed such American favourites as Virginia ham and hot dogs and visited with Eleanor and Franklin D. Roosevelt and the President's mother, Sara Delano Roosevelt.

treated to dinners, coffees, banquets and troupes of Norwegian-American folk dancers. They gave countless speeches, laid wreaths on innumerable monuments, and admired endless views. They rode to the bottom of the Grand Canyon and swam in chilly western streams. They traversed America's breadth and did more to cement American-Norwegian friendship and solidarity than countless diplomats and treaties.

The crown prince and princess' tour of America was a great success both for them personally and for Norway.

The America tour covered 29 American states in 69 days, during which time Crown Prince Olav was called upon to perform many a well-intentioned PR request. This he always did gracefully, although some of the occasions were not without their humour, as when he donned a full-fledged cowboy outfit at Glacier Park, Montana for the benefit of the press.

Despite the tragic loss of Queen Maud only months before, they never let the public down. They carried through their rigorous program with smiles on their faces. When the young Danish Prince Carl was elected king of Norway in 1905, he chose the motto 'All for Norway!' When Olav followed in his father's footsteps in 1957, he chose the same motto. Father and son have never denied Norway their *all* in any way.

The role of the royal family in Norway is strictly limited by the Norwegian constitution. Although at one time the king of Norway (and Sweden) exercised considerable personal power, this is no longer the case. When H.M. Haakon VII accepted the Norwegian throne, he did so with the understanding that his role as monarch would be to serve, to the best of his abilities, the good of the country and its citizens.

How the people are best served is traditionally defined by the party in power. Given this structure, King Haakon's first years were spent serving and supporting the prevailing party and/or parties – which usually meant the non-socialist parties. In January 1928, however, the same year that Josephine Baker visited Norway, and Oslo opened its underground, a turnabout occurred. King Haakon VII stepped beyond the limited role he had previously played to resolve an election stalemate that threatened to plunge Norway into political chaos.

By so doing, he broke the tradition of Conservative rule in Norway. After considerable negotiations with both interested sides, he assisted the Norwegian Labour Party, which was the party of the majority, to come into power. It was an unprecedented action on the part of the king, but one that won both peace for the country and respect for the monarchy. It demonstrated the influence a good king could have, especially in a time of national unrest. H.M. King Haakon's action during that cabinet crisis was a perfect example of how an impartial monarch with restricted powers could serve his country when motivated solely by the welfare of the nation.

For many, the Norwegian monarchy has come to represent Norway's very identity. This has never been more true than during World War II, when the exiled royal family stood in every true Norwegian's heart as the symbol of the free homeland.

THE WAR YEARS

An unprepared Norway was invaded on April 9, 1940. The royal family and the government were forced to flee the capital at dawn with both the German army and air force in determined pursuit. When asked to capitulate, several parliament members vacillated in uncertainty, but the king did not hesitate. 'No!' was his emphatic response.

At the king's express wish, Crown Princess Märtha and the three children were taken into neutral Sweden. Despite many efforts to keep both their presence and whereabouts secret, however, they were constantly forced to be on the move. Spies and German sympathizers were everywhere, and Märtha's and the children's safety was always feared for. America's President Roosevelt had offered his country as refuge for the royal family should the prevailing winds of war come to a head. When war erupted, he renewed his offer. On August 16, 1940, the crown princess and her three children boarded the *American Legion* bound for America.

For the three children from Norway, life in America was quite a change. Prince Harald and his two sisters had grown up in a very special and protected environment at Skaugum. Family albums overflow with pictures of the two girls, often beribboned in matching dresses, animatedly in play, their little brother in knickers and knee socks not far off. They were the crown prince and princess' children, recognized and beloved by all. While they didn't actually become 'Americanized' in America, there was a period when Harald's favourite song was 'Praise the Lord and pass the ammunition,' and years later Eleanor Roosevelt would tell an anecdote about the day when she had to save a prize stallion from an energetic little six-year-old trying

In August 1940, Crown Princess Märtha and the three royal children were evacuated to America for the duration of the war. During their exile, the crown princess worked relentlessly for the war effort, often broadcasting appeals for transmission both at home and abroad. Here, together with her children, autumn 1941.

to climb one of its hind legs with the admonition, 'Harald, a horse has dignity!'

Crown Princess Märtha and the children first stayed in New York's Waldorf Astoria Hotel before moving into the Roosevelt's private home at Hyde Park. They were eventually able to settle into a home of their own a short drive outside of Washington D.C. close to Bethesda, Maryland – Pook's Hill. There the children started school, and Crown Princess Märtha worked for the war effort. She was especially active in the Red Cross, an organization her father had faithfully served. Summer holidays were mostly spent in New England.

During the five long and difficult years the family was separated, Crown Princess Märtha was the very model of courage and optimism. She gained the deepest respect of those around her, and later, after her death, Eleanor Roosevelt was to say of her, 'We in this country will not forget Princess Märtha. She will always mean to us the finest qualities that a woman can have – courage, patience, kindness and generosity.'

When Crown Princess Märtha and the children were evacuated to Sweden, Crown Prince Olav and King Haakon VII remained behind in Norway. The plan called for the establishment of a base from which the Nazi invasion could be fought, but the royal party was continually harassed by air attacks, and all efforts to establish a camp were unsuccessful. On April 28, under heavy bombing, the king, crown prince and their party, together with 23 tons of gold from the Bank of Norway, were loaded onto a British cruiser at Molde enroute for northern Norway.

A few days later they transferred to the Norwegian ship *Heimdal*, the very same ship that had carried the royal family to Norway thirty-five years before. They were put ashore at Tromsø and there managed to establish a camp of sorts. By the end of May, it became apparent that a stand in Norway would be impossible. With heavy hearts, King Haakon VII and Crown Prince Olav boarded the English ship *Devonshire* on June 7, 1940 bound for England, which was still mourning the recent tragedy of Dunkirk. They remained in England throughout the war, overseeing the Norwegian war effort.

It was often said that June 7, 1940, the day the king was forced to leave Norway on board the *Devonshire*, was the most sorrowful day in his life. Crown Prince Olav had proposed that he remain behind in Norway, but both his father and the Cabinet refused. In the end, it was the belief of many that by evacuating Norway, the royal family and the government had actually preserved Norway and her

One of Norway's most famous press photos of H.M. King Haakon VII and Crown Prince Olav, taken during eight heavy days of bombing in Molde during the invasion of Norway, April 1940. The picture of father and son forced to seek shelter moved the Norwegian author Nordahl Grieg so deeply that two years later, in August 1942, he wrote one of modern Norway's most popular and patriotic poems, entitled simply 'The King'. Its opening lines read: 'Thus our King shall live before us:/By a white and silvery birch-stem,/'Gainst the dark of springtime pinewood,/Standing, with his son beside him,/Lone, while German planes fly over.' (translated by G.M. Gathorne-Hardy).

constitution. Norway may have been occupied, but she never submitted.

King and crown prince were met at Euston Station by King George VI, Winston Churchill, and Lord Halifax and taken directly to Buckingham Palace. They resided there until forced out by the heavy bombing raids. For years afterwards, the palace staff remembered the unusual calm and good-naturedness of 'the gentlemen,' King George and King Haakon. One night, a German bomb made a direct hit on the palace, and water from a broken pipe poured through the ceiling onto King Haakon as he lay in bed. A concerned King George came running to check on his uncle's safety. 'I'm fine,' remarked King Haakon, 'but you had better lend me an umbrella before Hitler sends his next greeting.'

They were eventually moved to Bowdown House, by Newbury in Berkshire. They lived there for two years until the house was requisitioned for the war effort by the air force. At that time, they moved closer to London, to a house belonging to one of the owners of the famous British chain 'Marks and Spencer,' and resided there for the duration of the war.

Father and son worked tirelessly for the war effort. They met with Norwegian seamen and soldiers, coordinated war-time activities, broadcast appeals to occupied Norway, and kept the wheels of the Norwegian government-in-exile turning. During their very first weeks in London, Crown Prince Olav gave a radio speech directed towards the 1,024 ships of the Norwegian Merchant Marine that was one of the most inspirational speeches of the war. Its title was 'Norwegian Sailors do not Submit':

'I ask. . .of every Norwegian sailor who is still able to sail at liberty under the Norwegian flag, wherever he goes, to remember that it depends on him more than on anyone else whether we shall live to see the day when a happy people again lives within the borders of Norway, and when all those who are so barred from their own shores, for which they all yearn, can again be reunited with their dear ones in a free fatherland. . . . Norwegian sailors on all the seas and in all ports and all countries, do what you can in order that we may reach our goal. . . .'

Two years later, at the dedication of a new warship, the *King Haakon VII*, President Roosevelt was to refer to the extraordinary dedication of the Norwegian people in fighting the common enemy. The catchphrase of his speech was

Look to Norway!' Crown Princess Märtha stood bravely by the President's side.

Crown Prince Olav was able to spend Christmases with his family by combining visits with them with inspection tours of North-American Norwegian training camps, and Märtha made the perilous Atlantic crossing to be with her father-in-law on his 70th birthday in London. Otherwise, the war-torn family had to be content with letters and occasional personal messages carried by friends. King Haakon missed his daughter-in-law and grandchildren sorely. At the end of a visit by a message-carrying friend, the messenger added that as he had left the crown princess and her family in America, little Prince Harald had given him two hearty hugs 'to give to grandfather and father.' 'Well,' the king asked the messenger, 'Aren't I going to get my hug?'

Within Norway's borders, the knowledge that the Norwegian royal family was safe, working for the liberation of the country, brought patriotism to a peak. King Haakon VII's name and sign became the symbol of a free Norway. At great personal risk, children painted *'Leve Kongen'* (Long live the King!) on fences, walls, and doorways. *H7* was written on frosty windows in train compartments, with flowers and stones on hillsides, with skis and skipoles on white slopes. The king was an inspiration to Norwegians everywhere.

In July 1944, three-and-a-half weeks after 'D Day,' Crown Prince Olav was named Norwegian Chief of Defense. Ten long months later, Norway was liberated on May 8, 1945. On May 11, Crown Princess Märtha flew over to England to be by her husband's side. They had one short, happy hour together in Edinburgh before he left for Norway.

Crown Prince Olav arrived in the newly-liberated capital on May 13, 1945. He was greeted by a city in the throes of victory. He rode in an open motorcar through the streets to a thundering roar of cheers and shower of flowers. One of the more colourful heroes of the Norwegian Resistance

Mid-day on June 7, 1945, exactly five years after their enforced evacuation of Norway, Crown Prince Olav was able to welcome his father, King Haakon VII, and family back home to a liberated Norway. The day also marked the end of the five-year separation the royal family had to bear on different sides of the Atlantic during the long war.

Movement, Max Manus, machine gun ready on his lap, rode guard.

High on the list of priorities was a stop at the royal palace. Although an attempt had been made to restore it to order, it was in total shambles. A few days later, when the crown prince had the opportunity to visit Skaugum, he found it, too, in total disarray. It had been occupied by a high-ranking Nazi who, at the end of the war, committed suicide in a nearby cave. Luckily, most of the original contents of the house were later found in a storage depot the Gestapo had used in town.

The king and crown prince had been forced to flee from Norway on June 7, 1940. June 7, 1945 seemed a propitious date to return. On a gray, wet, and misty morning, King Haakon, accompanied by his daughter-in-law and three grandchildren, sailed up Oslo fjord. Their ship was surrounded by thousands of small boats. At Drøbak the sea was so packed that it was said that one could step from deck to deck. A pilot came on board for the last part of the voyage and presented a bouquet of flowers to the crown princess. Crown Prince Olav joined his family to brief the king on the landing ceremony.

The streets were thick with people and flags. Not a face in the city was without a tear in its eye or a smile on its face, including the king's. Paal Berg, leader of the Norwegian resistance movement, formally welcomed the king home. A visibly moved crown princess peeked glimpses at her proud husband. The three royal children beamed up at their dignified father and grandfather. That evening, as the royal family stood on the palace balcony, over 100,000 Norwegians paid them tribute. Their faces revealed all the pent-up emotions of the past five years, now finally released in the joy of the day. The Norwegian royal family was home at last!

THE END OF AN ERA

King Haakon and Crown Prince Olav worked side-by-side during the busy post-war years. The devastation of the country affected both deeply, and it was clear that the rebuilding of the country would take many years. It was also clear, however, that the king was no longer able to sustain his relentless schedule of the past. He observed his seventy-third birthday two months after the family's return to Norway, and although he was as conscientious as ever, the crown prince stepped in to assist with the ever-growing duties of the monarchy whenever possible.

On August 3, 1947, on a beautiful cloud-free day, H.M. King Haakon VII celebrated his 75th birthday. The day was filled with well-wishers, and when the king was driven to and from a special service held at Vår Frelsers Church, hundreds of thousands of citizens paid him tribute. Among his congratulatory messages was one sent by five Norwegians and one Swede on a raft in the middle of the Pacific: the crew of the *Kon Tiki* on their epic expedition from the coast of Peru to Polynesia.

Among King Haakon VII's most memorable birthday presents was one given him by the people of Norway – the royal yacht *Norge*. A search for the perfect birthday present had been underway for several months, and when the king was approached with the idea, he was delighted. Fund-raising and the search for the perfect ship began at once, and a private yacht that had been used as an anti-submarine training ship during the war proved to fit the requisite specifications. The refurbished ship was formally presented to the king on June 9, 1948. Since that day it

Long, hard days of reconstruction lay before the Norwegian people after the end of the war in June 1945, and Crown Princess Märtha was often by her husband's side. New Year's Eve 1950 she broadcast a traditional New Year's Eve message to the Norwegian people, acknowledging the difficult years that lay behind and the goals still unfulfilled, encouraging the nation's citizens, and especially its women, to pursue in the goal of a rebuilt Norway.

has been in almost constant use by the royal family and is well-known to all of coastal Norway.

Eleanor Roosevelt paid a visit to the city of Oslo in the spring of 1950 to dedicate a statue in memory of her husband. That November, the crown prince and princess returned the visit. They visited President Truman, as well as carrying out the usual rounds of speeches, presentations, and receptions. Both were wonderful ambassadors for Norway, and Crown Princess Märtha won the hearts of the American press with her response to a reporter's question of what had impressed her most during their exhaustive tour. 'My husband,' she answered.

While Crown Prince Olav's stamina and energy has always been admired by those close to him, Crown Princess Märtha was never a strong woman. Like her mother-in-law, she had been plagued by migraines for a good part of her life and had suffered terribly with back problems after the war. It was clear that she had serious medical problems from the 1950s on, but she was a courageous and brave woman and did her best not to let them affect her life and duties more than was absolutely necessary. She was so ill in 1951 that she was not even able to attend her father's funeral.

In 1953 she again fell very ill, but determinedly made all the arrangements for both her son's confirmation and her daughter's wedding. She worsened rapidly that autumn and winter and despite persistent attempts to help her, passed away on April 5, 1954, at the age of fifty-three. Two weeks earlier, she and Crown Prince Olav had celebrated their 25th wedding anniversary in her hospital room.

A stained-glass window was dedicated and installed in Vår Frelsers chapel in memory of Crown Princess Märtha five months later. Other memorials were to follow. They are all testimony to the role Crown Princess Märtha held in the people's hearts. Norway's crown princess was a wonderful woman, admired and loved by all who came to know her. The entire nation went into mourning with the royal family at her death. Crown Prince Olav became a widower at the age of fifty and has never remarried.

Crown Princess Märtha lies buried in the same crypt as her mother-in-law, Queen Maud, below Akershus Fortress' chapel. Each year, on the anniversary of her death, H.M. King Olav V quietly pays his respects.

The year following Crown Princess Märtha's death, King Haakon's great-niece, Queen Elizabeth II, and her husband, Prince Philip, paid a state visit to Norway. It was the queen's first official visit to a non-Commonwealth country, and the preparations included a garden party for 1600 at the British Embassy, a gala performance of *Peer Gynt*, a formal dinner at the palace, lunch at Skaugum, and a dinner party on board the queen's yacht, the *Britannia*. The visit was a thorough success. A few weeks later, however, King Haakon fell and fractured his thigh. As is the case with many elderly people, it never healed properly, and he become immobilized. Two years later, he celebrated his eighty-fifth birthday quietly at home. He died soon thereafter, Saturday morning, September 21, 1957. In accordance with Norwegian law, Crown Prince Olav became king at the moment of his father's death.

It was King Olav V who called the prime minister with the news of King Haakon VII's death. The Cabinet was summoned to the palace within the hour. When assembled, King Olav made the announcement: 'It is my sad duty to have to inform the Cabinet that my beloved father, His Majesty King Haakon VII, died this morning at 4:35 a.m. In accordance with the Constitution, I have, as King of Norway, acceded to the Government, and I hereby take my written oath as prescribed under Article 9 of the Constitution. I shall bear the name of Olav V, and I adopt the same motto as my father chose: "All for Norway." '

King Haakon VII, Norway's first king as a modern independent nation, was laid to rest on October 2, 1957. Crown Prince Harald walked gravely by his father's side following his grandfather's coffin. He wore his military uniform as a newly-enrolled first-year cadet at the Military Academy. Four kings marched behind the bereaved son and grandson:

King Gustav VI Adolf of Sweden, King Frederik of Denmark, King Paul of Greece, and King Baudouin of Belgium. King Haakon's casket joined those of his wife, Queen Maud, and his daughter-in-law, Crown Princess Märtha, in the royal vault of Akershus Castle and Fortress.

H.M. KING OLAV V

There was no coronation ceremony for King Olav V. Norway had abolished coronation ceremonies in an amendment to the constitution in 1908. Although King Olav repeated his formal oath to the constitution in the Norwegian parliament on May 20, 1958, as head of the Norwegian Church, he felt a deep personal need to have the Church's blessing upon his succession. It was thus that on Sunday, June 22, 1958, exactly fifty-two years after his parents' coronation, King Olav V knelt alone at the railing in Trondheim's Nidaros Cathedral. His three adult children were among the 2,000 guests who witnessed the moving consecration ceremony.

Following Crown Princess Märtha's death, Princess Astrid, the youngest of the two princesses, assumed the role of first lady of the nation. Her sister Ragnhild was married and living in Brazil; her younger brother Harald was as yet unmarried. Following King Olav's consecration ceremony in Trondheim, she and her father toured southern Norway in the *Norge* before continuing back home to Oslo. The following year, they toured northern Norway. Both trips were immensely popular with the people and firmly cemented the agnomen 'The People's King' for H.M. King Olav V. He has continued such personal tours, and they are as popular today as they were twenty-five years ago. When he celebrated his 25th jubileum in 1982, he toured coastal Norway from Oslo to Kirkenes.

King Olav V has an easy, good-natured personality that has served him and Norway well these many years as crown prince and king. He may be the king, but he is also approachable and human. On his trip through northern Norway in

In the summer of 1959, H.M. King Olav V and Princess Astrid toured northern Norway. Princess Astrid's presence was a highlight of the tour for the local population; the last official visit by a female of Norway's ruling house had been Queen Maud's visit in 1930 when Stiklestad had celebrated its 900th anniversary. The king was popular, but oh how heads strained to see his daughter!

1958 he stopped to chat with a 91-year-old resident of an old-age home. When the king offered the compassionate comment that ninety-one was a good age, he was told, 'A little *too* good, you mean, king.' King Olav V served Norway for 52 years as its crown prince before becoming king. Practise has made perfect.

What does a modern king of Norway do? He represents his country both at home and abroad. He receives visiting heads of state and opens the Norwegian parliament each autumn. He presides over the weekly Cabinet meetings at the palace each Friday. After each election, it is the king who asks the departing prime minister who should be summoned to the palace to take the reins of Government. He

Always the sports enthusiast, King Olav V rarely misses Oslo's annual Holmenkollen Ski Championships. Here, congratulating Assar Rönnlund, the winner of the 50 kilometer cross-country race, 1968.

King Olav in his boat Norna X in a regatta near Copenhagen, 1966.

is Commander-in-chief of the armed forces and keeps a close watch on Norway's role in NATO. It is under his name that a great number of formal documents and decrees are issued, each requiring his personal signature. He holds four formal dinners a year: three for members of the *Storting*, the Diplomatic Corps, and the Supreme Court – with spouses – and one annual gentlemens' dinner for the bishops of the Norwegian Church. He also reads through the various appeals sent him as every citizen's right.

A modern king of Norway also skis, sails, reads, takes walks in the country, slips out of the palace to buy his own Christmas presents, and rides on public transportation when there is an energy crisis. He also lives a very private life as father, grandfather, and most recently, great-grand-father.

THE NEW GENERATION

The autumn following the liberation, Prince Harald, clad in knickers and tie, parents by his side, started at Smestad School. Attending Norwegian primary school with boys of the same age was a treat not granted his father, Crown Prince Olav, but the war had broken down many of the old traditions and patterns.

Everyone in the school knew who the new freckle-faced student was, but after a few hesitant weeks, Harald was accepted as just another classmate. He was a polite and well-mannered little boy, which made him popular with his teachers, and lively enough to make him sought-after as a friend. Several of his essays had to do with one of his favorite boyhood pastimes – sailing. Early reports also noted that he had a fine singing voice.

Upon graduating from primary school, Harald was enrolled in Oslo's oldest school, founded in 1152, 'Katedralskolen.' On August 21, 1950, Prince Harald, accompanied by his father, joined six of his Smestad classmates and nineteen new students to form Class Ia. Secondary school brought a new experience into Harald's young life – girls. Although he had two elder sisters, his classroom at Smestad School had been all-male.

Whether his above-average singing voice won him any female admirers during these years is unknown – his classmates have been far too discreet to give away any such secrets – but it is said that he did sing at least one solo at a school event during his years at 'Katedralskolen'.

Can life be normal for a young prince even if attending a local school? Probably not. Although his special status was only marked on his birthdays (by flying the flag), there

The royal family, together with family and personal friends, at Sikkelsdalen, in the 1950s: Princess Ragnhild (2nd from left), Princess Astrid (4th from left), H.M. King Haakon VII, Crown Prince Olav, Prince Harald, and Crown Princess Märtha. 'We are a ski family,' King Haakon once said.

probably weren't many of his classmates who were made honorary Crow Indians – as Harald was – when an American Indian dance troupe visited Oslo in 1953, and when he celebrated his eighteenth birthday in 1955, the entire school joined in.

Norwegian students spend their last month prior to graduation from secondary school as *russ*. Most students regard these few weeks as among the most memorable of their lives. The time symbolizes the last crazy days of childhood, and parties, parades, and parodies on society are the norm. Harald was as active a *russ* as any, and like his class-

75

mates had his school insignia, a red and white cat, stitched onto his jacket lapels, sported a student cap, and waved the traditional switch as merrily as any. In Oslo, the royal family traditionally stands on the palace balcony on the 17th of May to receive the thousands of school children who parade past. That year, Harald joined his classmates marching down Oslo's main streets, and hosted that evening's party at Skaugum. He graduated on June 22, 1955, with his upper secondary school diploma in science.

At the end of summer vacation, Prince Harald matriculated with 1,092 other students at the University of Oslo. He passed the general preliminary examination required of all University students in Norway before further specialization, but a University of Oslo degree was not in Prince Harald's future. Instead, that January he entered the Norwegian Cavalry Officers' Candidate School at Trandum to fulfill his sixteen months active military service. From there he continued on to the same Military Academy his father had attended thirty-six years earlier.

Attending the Military Academy was a natural step for Prince Harald to take. His grandfather, King Haakon, had been trained as a naval officer, and his father, Crown Prince Olav, had also pursued a military career. King Olav was to say of both his own and his son's training: 'We have had ample opportunity to be grateful to the Academy for the military training, command of discipline and understanding of the true meaning of good comradeship that we received there.'

Prince Harald entered the Military Academy on August 20, 1957 and graduated two years later, on August 28, 1959, with the rank of lieutenant. One of the first to congratulate him at his graduation ceremony was his date for the graduation ball, a perky short-haired girl he had met at a private party two months before, Miss Sonja Haraldsen.

A NEW MONARCH'S TRAINING

Although Prince Harald had accompanied his father and grandfather on official occasions before his graduation, his grandfather's death and father's investiture service marked the beginning of a new era and Crown Prince Harald's increasing official responsibilities.

He attended his first Cabinet meeting, together with his father, on September 27, 1957, six days after his grandfather passed away. Above his shoulder, on his left, hung the famous painting of Christian Michelsen welcoming his grandfather on board the *Heimdal* more than a half century before. Five months later, on February 21, 1958, his twenty-first birthday, he swore his oath of allegiance to the Norwegian Constitution as his father had done on his twenty-first birthday: 'I promise and swear to reign in accordance with the Constitution and the Laws, so help me Almighty and Omnipotent God.' Later that summer he accompanied his father to Trondheim for King Olav's special investiture service at the Trondheim Cathedral.

Therein began a hectic decade for Norway's crown prince. One month after paying an official visit to the U.S. where he met with both President Eisenhower and Eleanor Roosevelt, the crown prince began his studies at Balliol College, Oxford. As his father before him, he studied 'Modern Greats' – Oxfordese for economics, political science and history. He quickly became interested in rowing and by the summer of 1961 was in the Balliol first eight. The Boat Club, with its demanding training program, was the only club he joined during his years at Oxford. He was so committed to rowing that he missed the annual Hankø regatta back home in favour of the Henley Royal Regatta in England. (His father borrowed his boat, the *Fram II*, and won!) Crown Prince Harald concluded his studies in June of 1962, and returned to Balliol together with his father, a fellow alumnus, in 1963 to join in the college's 700th birthday celebrations.

Career responsibilities in the military kept Crown Prince Harald busy enough during this period (he held the rank of Captain in both the Army and Air Force and Lt. Captain in the Navy), but he always tried to find time for his favorite recreation – sailing. Few realized that the handsome Norwegian flag-bearer at the 1964 Summer Olympics in Tokyo, who also placed 8th in the 5.5 meter sailing event, was Norway's crown prince himself. The next year he was off on another major American and Canadian state visit.

Unbeknownst to most of Norway was the fact that the crown prince had fallen in love.

A NEW CROWN PRINCESS FOR NORWAY

When Crown Prince Harald was just four months old, another baby entered the world. Her name was Sonja Haraldsen, born on July 4th, 1937. Her birth was an especially joyful event for the Haraldsen family as they had lost a son the year before in a drowning accident and hoped that the new baby would help fill the void in their hearts.

Sonja Haraldsen first saw the crown prince when they were both seven years old. He was riding through the streets with his family, and she was standing in a brownie uniform on a street corner. It was the incredible 7th of June 1945

Sonja Haraldsen, at the age of four, in 1941—the girl who was to capture Crown Prince Harald's heart.

79

when all of Oslo had turned out to welcome the royal family back home to Norway after their war-time exile.

It wasn't until many years later that Sonja and Harald actually met one another, but meanwhile, another royal romance was in the air. Riding through the city with Prince Harald and his parents that same beautiful June day were his two sisters – Princess Ragnhild and Princess Astrid. At fourteen, Princess Ragnhild was the oldest of the three children. She had been the firstborn, the first royal child born in Norway since the Middle Ages. Princesses are supposed to marry princes, but it was Erling Lorentzen, a handsome 22-year-old escorting the royal family's *cortège* that day, whom she fell in love with. Eight years later, on May 15, 1953, the crown prince gave away his eldest daughter in marriage. The ceremony was held in Asker, and the reception at Skaugum.

Eight years later, Princess Astrid, who had served Norway for many years as first lady of the country, was joined in holy wedlock to a close friend of the family, Johan Martin Ferner. They were married on January 12, 1961 in the same Asker Church where Princess Ragnhild had been married.

Harald and Sonja's first face-to-face encounter oddly enough didn't occur in Oslo, where they attended neighbouring schools (Smestad and Slemdal), but at Hankø, a coastal Community, when they were both thirteen. During the summers, the royal family spent most of their time at Hankø, where they had their own summer home and could participate in the annual regatta. Sonja was enrolled at a sailing camp. One day someone ran by and snatched at her scarf. It was Prince Harald. No words were exchanged, and another nine years passed before they met again.

Sonja's childhood was spent as most other Norwegian childhoods. She attended her neighbourhood school and played with her friends and classmates in the afternoons. She spent summers together with her family at their summer house on one of Norway's most beautiful coastal shorelines, Tjøme, and Easter vacations skiing in the mountains. In 1950, the same year the crown prince and princess visited America, Sonja's parents also visited America, and brought back for their daughter an embroidered blouse and shell necklace. (She still has the necklace.) She was a joyful, pretty, and popular schoolgirl and never lacked companionship or activities.

After receiving her Lower Secondary School diploma in 1954, the school-weary young girl decided to try her hand at something new. She applied for a one-year program in dress design and sewing at Oslo Vocational School and was accepted. From there she set her sights on a special design school in Lausanne, Switzerland. She was only 17-years old when she left for Switzerland, and had a rough (and cold) settling-in period, but she stuck it out and eventually came to love her two years there. Next on her agenda was an Oslo business school and a residential language program in England. She celebrated her twenty-first birthday in an English pub together with fellow members of the Cambridge University Water Ski Club!

Nineteen fifty-nine found Sonja back home in Oslo, working in her father's clothing shop. This had been her career goal, but it was obvious that it wasn't enough for the bright and industrious young woman. Sonja had been growing restless and had been undecided about her future when a family tragedy struck. Her father died suddenly in March. She cancelled all thoughts other than staying at home by her mother's side.

She led a quiet life that spring, helping her mother in the garden and keeping her company. She had limited her activities, but accepted an invitation to a party a close friend was giving. There was another guest that evening who was to change her life – Crown Prince Harald. After a few casual conversations and get-togethers during the summer, he asked her to his graduation ball at the Military Academy.

Thus began nine long and difficult years. Crown Prince Harald was one of Europe's most eligible bachelors. His name had been linked with almost every one of Europe's unmarried princesses. The very day after he graduated from the Military Academy, the Greek royal family visited for four days. There were many excited whispers linking the young people of the two related families, and the Greek Princess Irene was a favourite candidate.

Everywhere Crown Prince Harald travelled, the press was busy predicting possible alliances. Which princess would he choose? It had to be a princess, that much was given. Prince Harald was Norway's crown prince. The two princesses might be allowed to marry commoners and become 'Princess Ragnhild Mrs. Lorentzen,' and 'Princess Astrid Mrs. Ferner', as decreed by their grandfather, King Haakon VII, but they were not destined to sit on the Norwegian throne.

Since the 1960s, at least three kings or crown princes have married commoners – King Baudouin of Belgium to Fabiola, Crown Prince Carl Gustav of Sweden to Silvia, and the Prince of Wales to Lady Diana – but these marriages had not broken the way for Norway's crown prince and his intended. In the 1960s, a marriage between a European crown prince and a commoner was unheard of.

During these painful years, Sonja kept busy. She travelled and learned foreign languages. She studied art history and lived and worked in both England and France while Harald attended royal weddings, official openings, and state funerals. Despite efforts on both their parts to keep their friendship private, Sonja's name began to appear in both local and foreign newspapers. It became apparent that their relationship was more than passing. It also became apparent that Norway's crown prince was unhappy.

H.M. King Olav V was in a difficult position, torn between his two roles as king and father. According to Norwegian law, a prince of the royal house must not marry without the king's permission or he loses his right to the throne. The issue was not so simple, however, and there were many long and serious conferences between King Olav V and his government and Cabinet before he felt able to accede to the young people's wish. On March 19, 1968 the Norwegian parliament was informed of King

On August 29, 1968 a radiant bride sat between her new father-in-law, H.M. King Olav V, and her husband, Crown Prince Harald, as Norway's new first lady. In the words of H.M. King Olav, she had 'entered Oslo Cathedral as Miss Sonja Haraldsen and had emerged as Norway's Crown Princess'.

Olav's consent to the betrothal of the Norwegian crown prince to Miss Sonja Haraldsen. The Norwegian radio station interrupted their regular 11:00 a.m. news broadcast with the incredible announcement. Sonja was in a beauty parlour at the time. When she left, she was met at the door by her new bodyguard.

For the second time in history (the first was when Crown

Prince Olav returned to Norway in 1945), the doors of the royal palace were thrown open to the press. The engaged couple handled the seasoned reporters like pros, and then promenaded through the palace grounds hand-in-hand for professional and amateur photographer alike. Their obvious happiness melted even the severest of critics.

They were married five months later, on a warm summer evening, August 29, 1968, in Oslo Cathedral. His Majesty King Olav himself gave the bride away. Nine hundred guests, including four kings, one queen, and two presidential couples, were among the guests in the church as millions watched on television.

King Olav V enjoys commenting that his family has become so thoroughly Norwegian that all have married Norwegian commoners.

Crown Prince Harald and his new bride combined a leisurely honeymoon with the 1968 Summer Olympics in Mexico where the crown prince participated in the 5.5 meter class in sailing. They returned home that autumn and moved into Skaugum, a wedding present from the king, just before Christmas.

Thirty-six years before, on the day Crown Prince Olav and his family returned to Skaugum after the fire, the community had welcomed their new neighbours with a torchlight parade. Once again, the citizens of Asker welcomed a crown prince and his bride into their midst. A proud father-in-law, King Olav V, stood by his new daughter-in-law's side. Together, they read out the emblazoned welcome word, *'Velkommen.'*

The crown prince and princess make formidable workers for Norway. Their intense and full programs include all manner of activities, and their representational tours abroad for Norway have won them the well-deserved gratitude of not only the Norwegian government, but also Norwegian industry. In addition to numerous hostess duties and official responsibilities, the crown princess has also found time to become one of Norway's most conscientious patrons of the arts.

Norway's crown prince and princess spend many weeks out of each year representing Norway and Norwegian interests abroad. While formal receptions, lectures and presentations form the lion's share of their program, their travels have not been without personal memories. Crown Prince Harald and Crown Princess Sonja, November 1982.

THE GENERATION OF THE FUTURE

Norway's youngest royal princess was born early in the evening of September 22, 1971. The Norwegian broadcasting company interrupted their regular program with the news at 17:55. She weighed 3590 grams, was 50 cm. long, and was named Märtha Louise in honour of the paternal grandmother she would never have the joy of knowing, and her paternal great-grandmother, Queen Louise of Denmark, Haakon VII's mother. King Olav V was in the United States when his newest grandchild was born, but flew home a few hours later.

Two years later, just a few weeks after his grandfather celebrated his 70th birthday, a new prince was born. He is the youngest heir to the Norwegian throne. His birthday on July 20, 1973 is the third royal birthday in July: King Olav celebrates his on the 2nd, Crown Princess Sonja on the 4th, and Haakon Magnus on the 20th. When Prince Haakon Magnus becomes king, he will be Norway's eighth King Haakon.

Both children were christened in the family christening gown made by Princess Ingeborg of Denmark, King Haakon VII's sister. The first child to be baptized in it was Princess Ingeborg's eldest daughter, Princess Margaretha. Since then it has been used in all the family christenings in both Denmark and Norway. H.M. King Olav V's first great-grandson, baptized Olav Alexander on January 5, 1986, initiated the fourth generation to wear the gown in Norway.

Prince Haakon Magnus and Princess Märtha Louise attend regular schools and enjoy as many of the advantages young people growing up in Norway have at their dis-

Flags, ice-cream, and the royal family are among Norway's 'musts' on the most important national holiday of the year-the 17th of May. Rain or shine, the Norwegian royal family greets the marching children of the city as they parade past the royal palace at the top of Karl Johans Gate on the nation's Constitution Day.

posal, given their position. Prince Haakon Magnus is an enthusiastic soccer player, and Princess Märtha Louise is a dedicated young horsewoman. They spend their summers at 'Berget' in Tjøme, the summer house Crown Princess Sonja inherited from her father, and at 'Bloksberg' at Hankø, owned privately by King Olav V and used each year during the Hankø regatta. During the winter, the family skis, either in their immediate surroundings or at one of the winter ski chalets owned by the family. The crown princess is a licensed ski instructor, so the children have had the best possible of teachers and a talented grandfather to pattern themselves after.

87

Prince Haakon Magnus, Crown Prince Harald, Crown Princess Sonja and Princess Märtha Louise, seen during a photo session at their residence Skaugum outside Oslo, Christmas 1985.

Whenever possible, they accompany their parents on semi-official and private trips, such as the lighting of the Christmas tree given by Oslo to London each year in Trafalgar Square, and family weddings. The children have had English nannies since they were young, and speak fluent English. Queen Maud introduced the English custom of hanging up Christmas stockings on Christmas Eve, and her son, H.M. King Olav V continued it with his own children when they were young. Traditions are important to Norway's first family.

A few years ago the crown prince's family visited Fredensborg, the traditional home of the Danish royal house,

'Europe's parlour.' Visitors, including members of most of Europe's ruling houses, used to etch their names on the glass windowpanes. One of the first names Prince Haakon Magnus and Princess Märtha found was that of their grandfather's mother, 'Maud'. It had been carved into the glass nearly one century ago.

Time moves on. Governments come and go. The royal house and the Norwegian Constitution are the two permanent fixtures of the Norwegian state. Norwegians are at ease with their democratic monarchy, and they are proud of their royal family. They love nothing more than meeting H.M. King Olav V face-to-face on a snowy ski trail in the hills above Oslo or bumping into him in a downtown bookshop.

King Edward VII was right when he predicted that his daughter, then a young newly-married English princess, and his son-in-law, the second-born son of a Danish crown prince, would come to be loved and respected by the Norwegian people. Their descendants are no less loved.

A constitutional monarchy seems to suit Norway and its citizens, and the cry of the Norwegian people, 'Long live the king and his house!' is a heart-felt sentiment.

Major Works Consulted

Berg, Arno. *Bygdøy kongsgård: Haakon V – Haakon VII* Oslo: J.W. Cappelens Forlag, 1952.

Berggrav, Eivind. *Mennesket Dronning Maud.* Oslo: Gyldendal Norsk Forlag, 1956.

Bratteli, Randi & Sissel Lange-Nielsen. *Sonja: Norges kronprinsesse.* Oslo: H. Aschehoug & Co., 1983.

Dronning Maud's Julealbum: Kronprins Olav Ute og Inde. Christiania: H. Abels Kunstforlag, 1910.

Evensberget, Snorre & Roy Gulbrandsen, ed. *Harald og Sonja.* Oslo: Gyldendal Norsk Forlag, 1968.

Greve, Tim. *Haakon VII of Norway: Founder of a New Monarchy.* Translated from the Norwegian and edited by Thomas Kingston Derry. London: C. Hurst & Company, 1983.

Grønoset, Dagfinn. *Med Kong Olav mot nord.* Oslo: H. Aschehoug & Co., 1959.

Gulbrandsen, Roy. *Kong Olavs signingsferd.* Oslo: Gyldendal, 1958.

Gulbrandsen, Roy, picture ed. *Et år med kongen.* Oslo: Gyldendal Norsk Forlag, 1961.

Halling, Sigurd. *Olav, Norges kronprins. Festskrift i anledning av H.K.H. kronprins Olavs bryllup.* Oslo, 1929.

Hansen, Guttorm et. al. *Kongen og folket: En hyllest til kong Olav V.* Oslo: Hjemmets bokforlag a.s., 1984.

Harald, Prins av Norge. Oslo: Abels Kunstforlag, 1937.

Haugstøl, Harald. *Harald, Prins av Norge.* Oslo: Nasjonalhjelpen, 1947.

Hjelde, Gunnar. *Oscarshall.* Oslo: Dreyers Forlag, 1978.

Hølaas, Odd, ed. *Norge under Haakon VII.* Oslo: J.W. Cappelens Forlag, 1952.

H7. All for Norway! Published on the occasion of H.M. King Haakon's 70th Birthday August 3, 1942. London: The Royal Norwegian Government's Information Office. Augsburg Publishing House, Minneapolis, Minnesota, U.S.A., 1942.

Kronprins Olav og kronprinsesse Märtha. Oslo: Vor Tid Ekstranummer, 1929.

Kronprins Olav & Prinsesse Märtha: Et album til minne om bryllupsfesten. Oslo: Damm, 1929.

Lande, Harald og Åsa Gran. *Norges Konger og Dronninger i tusen år.* Oslo: J.W. Cappelens Forlag, 1945.

Lille Kronprins Olav: Barnevers. Kristiania, 1905.

Märtha: Norges Kronprinsesse 1929-1954: En Minnebok. Oslo: Gyldendal Norsk Forlag, 1954.

Med kronprinsparet på Amerikaferden. Oslo: Norsk telegrambyrå, 1939.

Mykland, Knut, ed. *Norges Historie.* Oslo: J. W. Cappelens Forlag A.S., 1978.

Møst, Annemor & Roy Gulbrandsen, ed. *Familien på Skaugum.* Oslo: Gyldendal Norsk Forlag, 1971.

Møst, Annemor, et. al., ed. *Kongen møter folket.* En VG bok. Oslo: Schibsted, 1982.

Normann, N. *Med Kongen Ute og Hjemme: Hundre historier samlet og gjenfortalt.* Oslo: Gyldendal Norsk Forlag, 1957.

Seip, Didrik Arup, ed. *Haakon 7. Utgitt til 75-årsdagen 3. august 1947 av den norske regjeringen.* Oslo: Den norske Forleggerforening, 1947.

Olav, Kronprins. *Norwegian Sailors Do Not Submit: A radio address.* New York, 1940.

Olav V, Norges Konge. 2. juli 1963. 60 år. Oslo: Aas & Wahl, 1963.

Sommerfeldt, W. P., ed. *Hans Majestet Kong Haakon VII Taler 1905-1946: Et utvalg og en bibliografi.* Oslo: Nasjonalhjelpen til frihetskampens ofre, 1947.

Syvertsen, Brita, ed. *Et år med kronprinsfamilien.* Oslo: Williams forlag a.s., 1975.

Trekløveret på Skaugum. Oslo: Abels Kunstforlag, 1938.

Vår konge. Oslo: Nasjonalforlaget A.s., 1963.

Vår Konge og hans hus: Nord-Norgeferden og andre begivenheter i 1959. Oslo: Gyldendal Norsk Forlag, 1959.

Wedel Jarlsberg, F. *1905: Kongevalget.* Oslo: Gyldendal Norsk Forlag, 1946.

Wig, Kjell Arnljot. *Kongen ser tilbake.* Oslo: J.W. Cappelens Forlag A.S., 1977.

Wig, Kjell Arnljot. *Spillet om tronen.* Oslo: J.W. Cappelens Forlag A.S., 1980.

Østgaard, N. R., ed. *Olav: Norges konge.* Oslo: Gyldendal Norsk Forlag, 1957.

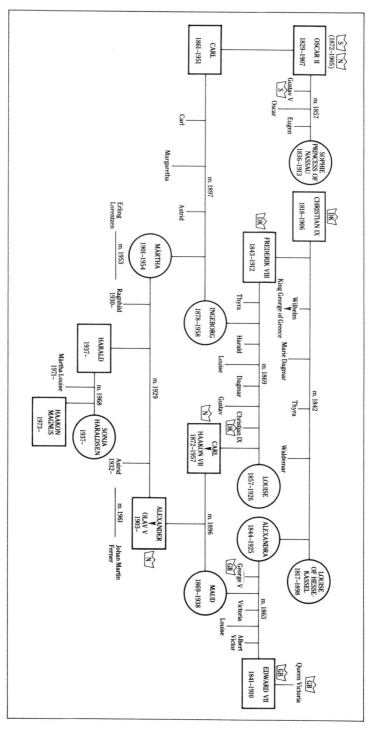

Family Chart for the Norwegian Royal Family.

KINGS AND QUEENS OF NORWAY

Readers are reminded that a certain degree of uncertainty surrounds several of the earliest entries (especially dates) given in this chart. It is meant to serve only as a general reference for the non-specialist and is not to be taken as the definitive list of Norway's kings and queens, their reign years, or life spans. *Author.*

Norway 900–1380

Harald Fairhair (Hårfagre), king of Norway approx. 900-940 A.D. married Ragnhild Eiriksdatter (Danish, dates unknown)

Erik Bloodaxe (Erik I, Blodøks), king of Norway approx. 940-945 married Gunnhild Gormsdatter (Danish, 900 ?-?)

Haakon the Good (Haakon I), king of Norway approx. 945-960

Harald Graypelt (Harald II), king of Norway approx. 960-970

Earl Haakon, king of Norway approx. 970-995

Olav Trygvason (Olav I), king of Norway 995-1000 married Thyra Haraldsdatter (Danish, dates unknown)

Earls Erik and Svein, kings of Norway 1000-1016

Olav Haraldson (St. Olav, Olav II), king of Norway 1016-1030 married Astrid Olavsdatter (Swedish, dates unknown) in 1019, queen of Norway 1019-1030?

Canute the Great (Prince Svein Alfivason regent), 1030-1035

Magnus the Good (Magnus I), 1035-1047

Harald Hardråde (Harald III), 1047-1066 married Ellisiv Jaroslavdatter (Russian, 1025 ?-?) approx. 1045, queen of Norway 1047-1066

Olav the Peaceful (Olav III Kyrre), 1066-1093 married Ingerid Svendsdatter (Danish, dates unknown) in 1063, queen of Norway 1066-?

Magnus Bareleg (Berrføtt, Magnus III), 1093-1103 married Margreta Fredkolla (Swedish, 1085-1130) in 1101, queen of Norway 1101-1103

Øystein Magnusson (Øystein I), 1103-1123 married Ingebjørg Guttormsdatter (Norwegian, dates unknown)

Sigurd Magnusson the Crusader (Sigurd Jorsalfare, Sigurd I), 1103-1130 married to Malmfrid Mstilavdatter (Russian, 1100?-1140?) in 1120, queen of Norway 1120-1130

Harald Gilchrist (Harald Gille, Harald IV), 1130-1136 married to

Ingerid Ragnvaldsdatter (Swedish, 1105?-1170?) approx. 1134, queen of Norway 1134-1136

Magnus Sigurdson the Blind (Magnus III), 1130-1138 married to Kristin Knudsdatter (Danish, 1117-?) in 1133, queen of Norway 1133-1138

Inge Haraldson (Inge I)

Sigurd Haraldson (Sigurd II), 1136-1161

Øystein Haraldson (Øystein II), 1142-1157 married to Ragna Nikolasdatter (Norwegian, 1150 ?-?), queen of Norway 1142?-1157

Haakon Sigurdson (Haakon II), 1161-1162

Magnus Erlingson (Magnus IV), 1163-1184 married to Eldrid (Norwegian, dates unknown), queen of Norway ?-1184

Sverre Sigurdson, 1184-1202 married to Margareta Eiriksdatter (Swedish, 1160?-1209?) in 1185, queen of Norway 1185-1202

Haakon Sverreson (Haakon III), 1202-1204

Inge Baardson (Inge II), 1204-1217

Haakon Haakonson (Haakon IV), 1217-1263 married to Margrete Skulesdatter (Norwegian, 1210?-1270) in 1225, queen of Norway 1225-1263

Magnus Haakonson the Lawmender (Magnus Lagabøte, Magnus V), 1263-1280 married to Ingeborg, daughter of Erik Plovpenning (Danish, 1243?-1287) in 1261, queen of Norway 1263-1280. (First queen to be crowned in Norway, ruled on behalf of her son 1280-87.)

Erik Magnusson (Erik II), 1280-1299 married to Margaret Alexandersdatter (Scotch, 1261-1283) in 1281, queen of Norway 1281-1283, thereafter to Isabella Bruce (Scotch, 1280-1358) in 1293, queen of Norway 1293-1299

Haakon Magnusson (Haakon V), 1299-1319 married to Eufemia of Ruppin (German, 1270?-1312) in 1299, queen of Norway 1299-1312

Magnus Erikson (Magnus VI), 1319-1355 (personal union with Sweden) married to Blanche of Namur (Netherlands, 1319?-1363) in 1335, queen of Norway 1335-1363

Haakon Magnusson (Haakon VI), 1355-1380 married to Margrethe Valdemarsdatter (Danish, 1353-1412) in 1363, queen of Norway 1363-1412.

Denmark and Norway 1380-1814

Olav Haakonson (Olav IV), king of Denmark and Norway 1380-1387

Queen Margrethe (see above),1387-1412

Erik of Pomerania (Erik III), 1389-1442 married to Philippa (English, 1394-1430) in 1406, queen 1412-1430

Christopher of Bavaria, 1442-1448 married to Dorothea of Brandenburg (German, 1429-1495) in 1445, queen 1445-1448

Christian I, 1448-1481 married to Dorothea of Brandenburg (see above), queen again 1450-1481

Hans, 1481-1513 married to Christine of Saxony (German, 1462-1521) in 1478, queen 1483-1513

Christian II, 1513-1523 married to Elisabeth (Spanish, 1501-1526) in 1515, queen 1515-1523

Frederik I, 1523-1533 married to Sophie of Pomerania (German, 1498-1568) in 1518, queen 1524-1533

Christian III, 1537-1559 married to Dorothea of Lauenburg (German, 1510-1517) in 1525, queen 1537-1559

Frederik II, 1559-1588 married to Sophie of Mecklenburg-Schwerin (German, 1558-1631) in 1572, queen 1572-1588

Christian IV, 1588-1648 married to Anna Cathrine of Brandenburg (German, 1575-1612) in 1597, queen 1597-1612

Frederik III, 1648-1670 married to Sophie Amalie of Braunschweig (German, 1628-1714) in 1643, queen 1648-1670

Christian V, 1670-1699 married to Charlotte Amalie of Hessen-Kassel (German, 1650-1714) in 1667, queen 1670-1699

Frederik IV, 1699-1730 married to Louise of Mecklenburg-Güstrow (German, 1667-1721) in 1695, queen 1699-1721, thereafter to Annie Sophie (Countess Reventlow) (Danish, 1693-1743) in 1721, queen 1721-1730

Christian VI, 1730-1746 married to Sophie Magdalene of Bayreuth (German, 1700-1770) in 1721, queen 1730-1746

Frederik V, 1746-1766 married to Louise (English, 1724-1751) in 1743, queen 1746-1751, thereafter to Juliane Marie of Braunschweig (German, 1729-1796) in 1752, queen 1752-1766

Christian VII, 1766-1808 married to Caroline Mathilde (English, 1751-1775) in 1766, queen 1766-1772

Frederik VI, 1808-1814 married to Marie Sophie Frederikke of Hessen (German, 1767-1852) in 1790, queen 1808-1814

Christian Frederik, King of Norway May 17-November 4, 1814

Sweden and Norway 1814-1905

Carl XIII, 1814-1818 married to Hedvig Elisabeth Charlotte (German, 1759-1818) in 1774, queen 1814-1818

Carl Johan (Bernadotte, Carl XIV Johan), 1818-1844 married to Desideria (French, 1777-1860) in 1798, queen 1818-1844

Oscar I, 1844-1859 married to Joséphine de Beauharnais (French, 1807-1876) in 1823, queen 1844-1859

Carl XV, 1859-1872 married to Louise (Netherlands, 1828-1871) in 1850, queen 1859-1871 (crowned in Trondheim August 5, 1860--first queen to be crowned in Norway since Queen Eufemia in 1299.)

Oscar II, 1872-1905 married to Sofie of Nassau (German, 1836-1913) in 1857, queen 1872-1905

Norway 1905 –

Haakon VII, 1905-1957 married to Maud (English, 1869-1938) in 1896, queen 1905-1938

Olav V, 1957- married to Märtha (Swedish, 1901-1954) in 1929
